AYAHUASCA ANALOGUES

AYAHUASCA ANALOGUES

Pangæan Entheogens

JONATHAN OTT

NATURAL PRODUCTS CO.
KENNEWICK, WA
1994

Other books by Jonathan Ott:

HALLUCINOGENIC
PLANTS OF NORTH AMERICA
(Wingbow Press, Berkeley, 1976,1979)

TEONANÁCATL: HALLUCINOGENIC
MUSHROOMS OF NORTH AMERICA
Co-Edited with J. Bigwood
(Madrona Publishers, Seattle, 1978,1985)

THE CACAHUATL EATER: RUMINATIONS
OF AN UNABASHED CHOCOLATE ADDICT
(Natural Products Co., Vashon, WA, 1985)

PERSEPHONE'S QUEST: ENTHEOGENS
AND THE ORIGINS OF RELIGION
Co-Authored with R.G. Wasson,
S. Kramrisch and C.A.P. Ruck
(Yale University Press, New Haven, 1986)

PHARMACOTHEON: ENTHEOGENIC
DRUGS, THEIR PLANT SOURCES AND HISTORY
(Natural Products Co., Kennewick, WA, 1993)

Forthcoming:
PHARMACOTHEON II: ENTHEOGENIC
PLANTS AND THE ORIGINS OF RELIGIONS

Design by Pablo Moya, typography by J. Ott
Obverse/Softcover: *Ashaninka Shaman Preparing Herbal Purges*
[detail] by Pablo Amaringo, 1992; slide by Luis Eduardo Luna
Verso/Softcover: *B. caapi* by C. Manuel Torres; *P. viridis* by J. Ott
Drawings: Title and colophon pages by Martín Vinaver;
Page 8 by Elmer W. Smith; page 32 by Irene Brady Kistler

ISBN 0–9614234–4–7 (hardcover) $30.00
ISBN 0–9614234–5–5 (paperback) $15.00

Sales: Jonathan Ott Books; Post Office Box 1251; Occidental, CA; USA 95465

TABLE OF CONTENTS

BANISTERIOPSIS *Caapi*

(Spruce ex Griseb.) Morton

1. Flowering branch; about half-size.
2. Flower; 2.5 times magnification.
3. Samara [fruit]; just over half-size.

EXORDIUM
The Amazonian Amrta and the Entheogenic Reformation

> How do you know but ev'ry Bird that cuts the airy way,
> Is an immense world of delight, clos'd by your senses five?
>
> **William Blake**
> *The Marriage of Heaven and Hell* (1793)

The rediscovery by R. Gordon Wasson of the traditional shamanic use of entheogenic[1] mushrooms in southern México in 1955, and Wasson's publication in *Life* magazine two years later of a popular article describing his "great adventure" partaking of the holy sacrament with Mazatec shaman María Sabina, engendered an astonishing revival of interest in shamanic inebriants [Wasson 1957; Wasson & Wasson 1957]. The entheogenic drug psilocybine, isolated from María Sabina's mushrooms by Albert Hofmann, together with LSD, a semi-synthetic mushroomic entheogen discovered serendipitously by Hofmann 12 years before Wasson lifted the veil of the holy mystery in México, went on to become key catalysts in an anachronistic international revival of archaic religion, which was destined to shake western society to its core [Horowitz 1991; Ott 1978]. The resulting "countercultural" movement of the "Psychedelic Sixties" marked an unprecedented departure from business as usual, setting the stage for a modern Entheogenic Reformation, which promises to evoke more radical and far-reaching changes in western religion than did its predecessor. Indeed, Martin Luther's 95 theses of October 1517 packed far less punch than did Gordon Wasson's *one* thesis 440 years later—for Wasson had peeled away the ossified accretion of many, many layers of symbol and dogma which enshrouded the core mystery in impenetrable obfuscation; had laid bare before the eyes of an astonished world, in all its dazzling quotidian humility, *the holy sacrament itself,* a sacrament which "carried its own conviction" and did not limp along encumbered by faith in an absurd Doctrine of Transubstantiation; a sacrament *which obviated the necessity of faith itself,* allowing every communicant to attest to "the miracle he has experienced" [Ott 1990; Wasson 1961].

Although María Sabina's mushrooms and psilocybine were the original inciters of this remarkable phenomenon, LSD was to emerge as the standard-bearer in the Entheogenic Reformation. For technical and economic reasons, LSD came to be

[9]

widely manufactured by the incipient underground chemical network jerry-built after the suspension of legal LSD manufacture in 1965 and the subsequent international proscription of this unique pharmacotheon. Indeed, this drug could be manufactured for about a penny a dose, even with the grossly inflated prices for starting materials and reagents which prevailed under the black-market conditions.[2] In part owing to a vigorous propaganda campaign against LSD by the governments of the United States and other countries, the drug's popularity waned as the sixties gave way to the seventies [Ott 1993]. Furthermore, as part of a "back-to-nature" movement, itself in large measure another consequence of the Entheogenic Reformation, a hard-core of established entheogen *aficionados* became more interested in phytoentheogens than in purified products of the chemical industry, however countercultural, and LSD was wrongly stigmatized as a "synthetic" (that is, artificial[3]) "chemical." This fact, combined with the introduction in 1975–1978 of reliable, low-technology methodology for small-scale cultivation of psilocybine-containing mushrooms [Harris 1976; Oss & Oeric 1975; Ott & Bigwood 1978] caused the focus of attention to shift back to psilocybine as the primary entheogen in countercultural circles [Ott 1993].Thus psilocybian mushrooms, especially *Psilocybe* [*Stropharia*] *cubensis*, became the entheogen of choice in the late seventies and early eighties, and LSD became ever more difficult to procure.

Toward the end of the 1980s, as a feature of the international ecological movement favoring tropical rainforest conservation, a movement which also had its roots in the Entheogenic Reformation, the continuing interest in entheogenic drugs began to focus ever more on *ayahuasca*, a pan-Amazonian entheogenic potion made from tropical rainforest plants [Ott 1993]. As the eighties became the nineties, *ayahuasca* was thrust ever more into the limelight as the new, modern, "hip" entheogen of the *cognoscenti*. By 1980 the phenomenon of "*ayahuasca* tourism" began to appear [Ott 1993], much as "mushroomic tourism" had followed Wasson's astonishing discoveries in México [Ott 1975,1976]. Few fragile surviving threads of preliterate spirituality in Amazonia, and the ephemeral "pharmacratic peace" [Escohotado 1989] which had seen *ayahuasca* overlooked in the contemporary crusade against shamanic inebriants, were gravely jeopardized by the sudden arrival in Amazonia of perfervid contingents of cosmopolitan *ayahuasca* tourists [Ott 1993].

Contemporary ethnobotany of *ayahuasca* is complicated by the fact that this shamanic inebriant, more so than any other entheogen we know, had managed to find a place for itself in the modern world long before its recent rediscovery by the entheogenic counterculture. Mestizo *ayahuasqueros* had continued to use the Amazonian *ambrosia* in urban areas of Perú and Colombia, even as their Indian forebears continued, in ever decreasing measure, to commune with *Sacha Runa* (the "jungle man") and other "plant spirits" in ever-diminishing islands of primary rainforest throughout Amazonia [Dobkin de Ríos 1970a,1970b,1972,1973,1992; Lamb 1974; Luna 1984a,1984b,1986c,1991; Luna & Amaringo 1991]. Furthermore, the last six decades have seen the growth of a remarkable syncretic Neo-Christian religion with *ayahuasca* as the sacrament. Following humble beginnings in the state of Acre in Brazilian Amazonia, these contemporary religious groups communing with *Santo Daime* or *Chá Hoasca* (as *ayahuasca* is known to them) have grown into major international religious movements with thousands of members [Centro 1989; Henman 1986; Lowy 1987; MacRae 1992; Prance 1970]. Far from being an aberration or anachronism, these churches, and the African Bwiti religion centered on the entheogenic sacrament *eboka* [Samorini 1992], rather represent the future of Christianity, stripped of its Doctrine of Transubstantiation by the Entheogenic Reformation, and with one or another *genuine* entheogen replacing the *placebo* sacrament!

The "mushroomic tourism" which followed on the heels of Wasson's penetration of the *arcanum arcanorum* in México profaned the wondrous mushrooms, which became ordinary articles of the tourist trade. Self-styled shamans staged spurious mushroom ceremonies for the eager tourists; the mushrooms themselves came to be widely and conspicuously sold like so many trinkets and souvenirs, contributing to the accelerated demise of the archaic cult [Ott 1975; Wasson 1977,1980]. Some shamans, like María Sabina, even served jail sentences in Oaxaca City for allegedly pandering to the mushroomic tourist trade [Estrada 1977]—rather like putting the Pope in jail for dispensing wafers and wine! Eventually, the popular dissemination of information on the abundance of the psilocybian mushrooms outside of México [Cooper 1977; Gartz 1993; Haard & Haard 1975; Menser 1977; Ott 1976,1978; Ott & Bigwood 1978,1985; Stamets 1978], combined with the above-mentioned introduction of home technology for the cultivation of psilocybian species [Harris 1976; Oss & Oeric 1975; Ott & Bigwood 1978,1985; Stamets & Chilton 1983] conspired to put an end to this unwelcome intrusion of outsiders, allowing the villages thus influenced to return to approximate normality, and distracting unwanted official attention away from the fungal pharmacotheon.

Ethnobotanical, pharmacognostical and pharmacological studies of *ayahuasca* commenced midway through the nineteenth century, and by the late 1960s had more or less elucidated the unique pharmacology of the jungle *amrta*,[4] which was found to be an ingenious *kykeon*[5] or amalgam of one plant infusion containing harmine and related enzyme-inhibitors with a second containing *N,N*-dimethyltryptamine (DMT), an entheogen ordinarily inactive orally [McKenna *et al.* 1984a;

Ott 1993]. Parallel phytochemical studies which will, along with the ethnopharmacognosy of *ayahuasca,* be summarized in this book, had meanwhile shown DMT and the *ayahuasca-*type natural enzyme-inhibitors (known technically as β-carbolines) to be far from rare—indeed, there are theoretically *several thousand possible combinations* of two plant extracts which could yield an entheogenic potion analogous to *ayahuasca.* These are the "*ayahuasca* analogues" of this book's title, which have also been called *ayahuasca borealis,* or the "northern *ayahuasca,*" to distinguish them from decidedly tropical Amazonian *ayahuasca,* which we would technically have to call *ayahuasca australis* [McKenna 1992]. As I researched *ayahuasca* for my recent book *Pharmacotheon* [Ott 1993], I realized that there were several *lacunæ* in scientific knowledge of the pharmacognosy of *ayahuasca,* and I embarked on an ambitious series of psychonautic experiments designed to elucidate the human pharmacology of this unique entheogenic potion. I endeavored not only to replicate the effects of *ayahuasca australis* with pure active compounds in "*ayahuasca* capsules" (*pharmahuasca*), but to provoke such an effect using readily-available plants from the temperate zone, some of which are actually more rational sources of *ayahuasca* from the chemist's perspective, as they contain much higher concentrations of DMT and β-carbolines than do their Amazonian prototypes. This book is the fruit of my field, library and laboratory research on the Amazonian *kykeon.*

It is my fervent hope that this book will contribute to the demise of *ayahuasca* tourism in Amazonia, which can only disrupt the evanescent remnant of preliterate religiosity struggling to make a place for itself in the modern world, while attracting the wrong kind of political attention to *ayahuasca.* Furthermore, inasmuch as I am implacably opposed to drug prohibition, and think that widespread contemporary use of entheogens constitutes the best ecological hope for humankind on the threshold of a new millennium—a new millennium which could be the start of a new Golden Age, or the continuation and dreadful culmination of a cataclysmic biological and cultural Holocaust—I hope the simple home technology described in this book will drive the last nail into the coffin of the evil and hypocritical, fifteen-hundred-and-ninety-eight-year-old crusade to eliminate this class of drugs from the face of the Earth. May the Entheogenic Reformation prevail over the Pharmacratic Inquisition, leading to the spiritual rebirth of humankind at Our Lady Gæa's [6] breasts, from which may ever copiously flow the *amrta,* the *ambrosia,* the *ayahuasca* of eternal life!

Jonathan Ott, F.L.S.
Ecuador–México–Spain
Spring 1992—Winter 1994

CHAPTER ONE
Natural History of Ayahuasca
A Pan–Amazonian Entheogen

In 1851 a young botanist named Richard Spruce was conducting botanical studies on the lower Río Vaupés in Amazonian Brazil, when a group of Tukanoan Indians from Urubú-coára, "The Place of the Buzzard," invited him to participate in a *dabocurí* feast, at which his hosts partook liberally of a "nauseous beverage" which they said provoked visions. The drink, *caapi*, was made from a vine, and Spruce drank a small cup of it, apparently insufficient to evoke much of an effect. But Spruce documented its effect on his Indian friends, and questioned them carefully about the (to him) novel entheogen. He was permitted to see the plant from which the *caapi* potion had been prepared, and he found it in full flower, enabling him to collect good voucher specimens, which he sent to Kew Gardens in England. Although there were scattered early mentions of this "diabolical brew" by Jesuit missionaries and others, Spruce was the first botanist to collect and identify the plant, which he had previously heard about from Brazilian mestizos, under the name *yajé*. He presciently collected material for eventual chemical analysis, and named the plant *Banisteria caapi* [Anon. 1855; Reichel-Dolmatoff 1975]. Seven years later, in the Ecuadorian Amazon drainage area of the Río Napo, the Ecuadorian civil servant Manuel Villavicencio described the peculiar effects of *aya-huasca*, a potion prepared from a vine by the Angatero, Mazán and Záparo Indians. Villavicencio appears to have been the first outsider to describe personally the full effects of the potion and how he "seemed to enter on an aerial voyage…" in which he saw "the most charming landscapes, great cities, lofty towers, beautiful parks, and other delightful things." Villavicencio published his account in 1858, fifteen years before Spruce's first paper on the Amazonian "narcotics"[7] [Spruce 1873; Villavicencio 1858]. Spruce, meanwhile, had observed in 1854 the use of *caapi* chewed "as some people do tobacco" by itinerant Guahibo Indians close to the Maipures Falls in the Orinoco River basin of Venezuela, and in 1859 encountered Villavicencio's *ayahuasca* in use among the Ecuadorian Záparo Indians. Spruce correctly concluded that *caapi, yajé* and *ayahuasca* were kindred potions prepared from *Banisteria caapi*, today known more commonly as *Banisteriopsis caapi* [Gates 1982], and his detailed notes were published posthumously [Spruce 1908].

Subsequent research has confirmed Spruce's vision of a pan-Amazonian entheogenic potion, the range of which he had personally established from the east in the area of the Río Negro in Brazil, west to the foothills of the Andes in Amazonian Ecuador, and north to the Orinoco basin of Venezuela. In the 135 years since the pioneering reports of Spruce and Villavicencio, the range of indigenous use of *ayahuasca*-type potions has been extended westward to the Pacific coastal areas of Colombia and Ecuador, where it is used under the names *pildé* and *dapa* by the Emberá and Noanamá Indians respectively. Such use is also found farther north, in coastal areas of Panamá [Reichel-Dolmatoff 1960]. Furthermore, this range has been extended greatly to the south, where its use has been widely documented in Amazonian Perú and Bolivia [Andritsky 1988; Baer 1969; Baer & Snell 1974; Dobkin de Ríos 1970a,1970b,1972,1973,1992; Friedberg 1965; Kensinger 1973; Kusel 1965; Luna 1984a,1984b,1991; Luna & Amaringo 1991; Rusby 1923; Siskind 1973; Weiss 1973; White 1922]. Rather detailed information is available from careful study of its use in the Colombian Amazon [Bristol 1966; Brüzzi 1962; Calella 1935,1944a,1944b; Goldman 1963; Koch-Grünberg 1909,1923; Morton 1931; Reichel-Dolmatoff 1944,1969,1970,1972,1975; Uscátegui 1959,1961]. We also have detailed information regarding indigenous use of *ayahuasca* in Ecuador [Davis & Yost 1983; Harner 1973a,1973b,1973c; Marles *et al.* 1988; Naranjo 1975,1979, 1983] and Brazil [Ducke 1957; Lowie 1946; Prance 1970; Prance & Prance 1970; Prance *et al.* 1977].The great ethnobotanist Richard Evans Schultes has clarified considerably the picture of *ayahuasca* ethnobotany in many detailed papers and superb books [Schultes 1957,1986b,1988; Schultes & Hofmann 1980; Schultes & Raffauf 1960,1990,1992]. Over this immense range, Luna has enumerated at least 72 indigenous groups reported to have used the potion [Luna 1986b] and has listed at least 42 known autochthonous names for the drug [Luna 1986c]. The best bibliographies to *ayahuasca* compiled so far run to over 300 sources [Luna 1986a; Luna & Amaringo 1991]. In this book the name *ayahuasca* will be used in reference both to the major source plant, *Banisteriopsis caapi* and to the entheogenic potions prepared from this and related species of Amazonian plants.

The botany of *ayahuasca* potions has been confused by a plethora of scientific names attached to plants reportedly employed in making the jungle *ambrosia*. While most reports make reference to Spruce's *Banisteriopsis caapi*, also commonly mentioned are *B. argentea, B. inebrians, B. longialata, B. lutea, B. martiniana, B. metallicolor, B. muricata, B. quitensis* and *B. rusbyana* [Schultes 1957,1986b]. Thanks to important and long-overdue taxonomic work by Bronwen Gates, the picture has clarified considerably. The most common "other" species of *ayahuasca, B. inebrians* and *B. quitensis,* are today regarded to be synonyms for *B. caapi* [Gates 1982]. Still accepted as "minor" source-plants for *ayahuasca* are *Banisteriopsis muricata* (by far the most widespread species in the genus, for which *B. argentea* and *B. metallicolor* are two of thirty-two synonyms) and *B. martiniana* var. *subenervia* (reported as *B. martiniana* var. *laevis*) [Davis & Yost 1983; García Barriga 1975; Gates 1982,1986; Schultes 1975]. The former, under the name *míi* or *sacha* ("wild") *ayahuasca* may be used as a weaker substitute for *B. caapi* by Witoto and Waorani Indians [Davis & Yost 1983], although the Waorani use has been said to be strictly symbolic and not pharmacologic [Miller 1993]. Additional *Banisteriopsis* species considered by Schultes to be sources of *ayahuasca* are *B. longialata* and possibly *B. lutea* [Schultes 1986b]. Some species of *Banisteriopsis* have ethnomedicinal uses apart from these entheogenic potions. *Banisteriopsis lucida* or *cají* is used in fishing magic in Venezuela [Boom & Moestl 1990], while in Brazil *B. argyrophylla* root decoction is used to treat kidney ailments [Schmeda Hirschmann & De Arias 1990]. The widely-reported *Banisteriopsis rusbyana,* today being classified as *Diplopterys cabrerana* [Gates 1986], is more precisely regarded as one of the principal *ayahuasca* additive or "admixture" plants, which will be treated in detail below.

Early reports by Spruce [1908] and Theodor Koch-Grünberg [1909,1923] made reference to different "kinds" of *caapi* in the Vaupés, and Schultes found that the Makú Indians of the Brazilian Río Tikié would prepare a *caapi*-like entheogenic potion from *Tetrapterys methystica,* also in the same Malpighiaceae family as *Banisteriopsis* [Schultes 1954a,1957; Schultes & Raffauf 1990], and the Karapaná Indians of the Colombian Río Apaporis similarly prepare an entheogenic potion from *Tetrapterys mucronata* [Schultes & Raffauf 1990]. Gates[1986] regarded *Tetrapterys methystica* to be synonymous with *T. styloptera.* Another species of Malpighiaceae, *Mascagnia psilophylla* var. *antifebrilis,* today known as *Callaeum antifebrile* (and also known by the synonyms *Banisteria antifebrilis* and *Cabi paraensis*) [Gates 1986] was reported as the basic ingredient of an entheogenic potion, but was part of a mixed collection containing also *Banisteriopsis* material [Schultes 1957]. Like *Diplopterys cabrerana,* this species is also more properly considered to be among *ayahuasca* admixture plants [Luna & Amaringo 1991]. One of the more obscure species of Malpighiaceae reported to be a basis for *ayahuasca* potions is *Lophanthera lactescens,* about which we know little [Schultes 1986b]. Widespread references in scientific literature to *Prestonia amazonica* or *Haemadictyon amazonicum* as *yajé* are the results of an unfortunate error, and there are no voucher specimens to support the inclusion of this species of Apocynaceae in the *ayahuasca* complex [Schultes & Raffauf 1960]. Similarly, *Brugmansia* species (which are important as *ayahuasca* additive plants, as we will see below) were wrongly stated by a missionary in the 1890s to be the main ingredient of an *ayahuasca* potion prepared by the Ecuadorian "Jívaro" Indians (this is a pejorative name for Shuar Indians and will not be used in this book) under the name *natema*. This involved an unfortunate confusion between *maikoa*, as the Shuar call the *Brugmansia* species (which they use in *ayahuasca*), and *natema* or *ayahuasca*. The genus *Aristolochia* was proposed in the identification of material of *ayahuasca* studied by Colombian chemist G. Fischer Cárdenas, and this wild guess has greatly confused the subsequent literature [Schultes 1957].

In summary, a recent paper by Gates [1986], representing the most conservative stance (that is, a minimum of species) on the number of malpighiaceous plants used as bases for *ayahuasca* potions, accepted the following species:

Banisteriopsis caapi	[=*B. inebrians, B. quitensis*]
Banisteriopsis muricata	[=*B. argentea, B. metallicolor, etc.*]
Callaeum antifebrile	[=*Cabi paraensis, Mascagnia psilophylla*]
Tetrapterys styloptera	[=*T. methystica*]

More liberal analysis of the literature would also include the following species reported as source plants for *ayahuasca* potions and accepted by Gates as valid taxa:

Banisteriopsis longialata	[=*Banisteria rusbyana*]
Banisteriopsis lutea	[=*Banisteriopsis nitrosiodora*]
Banisteriopsis martiniana var. *subenervia*	[=*B. martiniana* var. *laevis*]
Lophanthera lactescens	
Tetrapterys mucronata	

As we will see in Chapter Two, these species of Malpighiaceae are the sources of the harmine-type enzyme inhibitors important in *ayahuasca* pharmacology, and known to chemists as the β-carboline alkaloids.

Banisteriopsis caapi is a liana which grows in Amazonian lowland rainforests. It is found as far south as Bolivia, and as far north as Venezuela and Panamá. It grows in Amazonian Colombia, Ecuador, Perú and Brazil, and escaped over the Andes to coastal Ecuador. Inasmuch as it is widely propagated by cuttings for cultivation, it is difficult to establish a natural range. Amazonian groups recognize various "kinds" of *ayahuasca* within the botanical concept *B. caapi*, and these doubtless represent clones which are distinct chemical races of the plant [Gates 1982; Schultes 1986a]. *Banisteriopsis muricata* is a vining shrub or liana which has the largest range of any

[16]

species in the genus. It grows as far north as southern México, and as far south as Argentina, both in tropical rainforest and in semideciduous forest [Gates 1982]. *Banisteriopsis longialata* is a liana which grows in the Andes of Colombia, Perú and Bolivia; *B. lutea* is a vine growing in Argentina, Paraguay, Bolivia and Perú, extending to the east throughout Brazil; and *B. martiniana* var. *subenervia* is a liana from tropical rainforests of Amazonian Brazil, Perú and Colombia, extending to the upper Orinoco in Venezuela [Gates 1982]. *Tetrapterys styloptera* is a bush known from the Colombian Amazon [Schultes & Raffauf 1990]; and *Callaeum antifebrile* is a liana from Amazonian Perú [Gates 1986; Schultes & Raffauf 1990].

Ordinarily, *ayahuasca* potions consist of aqueous infusions or decoctions from wild or cultivated lianas of *Banisteriopsis caapi* and related species. There is scanty evidence for the use of *Banisteriopsis* species in South American entheogenic snuffs [Bernauer 1964; Holmstedt & Lindgren 1967; Ott 1993[8]], and unconfirmed reports of the use of *Banisteriopsis* infusions as a clyster or enema [De Smet 1983,1985; Emboden 1979; Furst 1976; Furst & Coe 1977]. Schultes also found that the Witoto Indians of Amazonian Colombia at times smoke dried leaves and "young bark" of *Banisteriopsis caapi*, wrapped into cigarettes with leaves of an unidentified *Heliconia* species [Schultes 1985b]. Nevertheless, by far the most common use of *ayahuasca* potions is by the oral route of administration.

In the preparation of *ayahuasca* potions, whole stems, longitudinally sectioned stems, stem shavings or pounded stems of the source lianas are extracted in water. Sometimes, as among the Tukano of the Colombian Vaupés, pieces of the lianas are macerated in a mortar, allowed to stand with cold water, then strained before ingesting the cold-water infusion [Reichel-Dolmatoff 1970]. This sort of "instant *ayahuasca*" is appealing in its simplicity, and we will recall that Spruce described the Guahibo Indians chewing dried *ayahuasca* stems like tobacco [Schultes & Raffauf 1992]. The similar practice of simply kneading the liana bark in cold water has been said to be the most common means of *ayahuasca* preparation in the Colombian Amazon [Schultes & Raffauf 1992]. The plants may also be extracted with hot water to prepare entheogenic potions. In some cases, for example among the Cashinahua, Sharanahua and Culina Indians in the Río Purús area of Amazonian Perú, the plant matter is heated in water for about an hour, filtered, cooled and summarily drunk [Der Marderosian *et al.* 1970; Rivier & Lindgren 1972]. In Amazonian Ecuador and nearby areas of northern Perú, there is a tendency to boil the plant matter in water for a prolonged period. At times the water may be boiled down, decanted, more water then added, further boiling followed by filtration and then prolonged simmering of the filtrate to concentrate it, with a total of 10–15 hours cooking time

[McKenna *et al.* 1984a]. This procedure is considerably more cumbersome and decidedly *not* energy-efficient. While heating would be expected to enhance the extraction of the *ayahuasca* alkaloids into water, there is evidence that the prolonged heating leads, as would be expected, to degradation of some of the active compounds. Harmaline, for example, which is an important secondary alkaloid of *Banisteriopsis* lianas, and appears to be one of the most active enzyme-inhibitors in the plants, seems to be largely or completely destroyed by the heating process, as we will see when we discuss *ayahuasca* pharmacognosy.

The resulting *ayahuasca* brews are ingested in a shamanic or ethnomedicinal context. While it has been suggested that the potions may be important as a sort of chemotherapy against parasitic worms [Rodríguez *et al.* 1982], by far the most important use of *ayahuasca* is as what Luna astutely called a "plant teacher"—the *ayahuasca* plant and potion is itself the teacher of the aspiring shaman [Luna 1984a, 1984b]. Accordingly, *ayahuasca* is of paramount importance in the apprenticeship of a neophyte *payé* or shaman. In preliterate cultures, the shaman, like the Aztec *pahini* ("who consumes medicine") ingests the pharmacotheon, the *medicamentum divinum*, in order to learn from this "plant teacher" the cause of the disease, the appropriate therapy and the prognosis. It is precisely as a result of the divine knowledge conferred on the healer by the plant teacher that such a practitioner is regarded to be a *shaman* [from Tungusian *saman*], *payé*, *yachaj*, or Mazatec *cho-ta-ci-ne*—"one who knows" [Ott 1993].

In the case of the Peruvian *ayahuasqueros*, the shaman also may learn *icaros*, supernatural melodies, from the plant [Giove 1992; Luna 1984a,1984b]. It was suggested that the *icaros* are synæsthetically transmogrified *ayahuasca* visions [Bellier 1986; Gebhart-Sayer 1986; Siskind 1973]. Images derived from *ayahuasca* visions are a prominent feature of Amazonian art [Reichel-Dolmatoff 1971,1972,1975, 1978]. The magical melodies and *ayahuasca*-inspired art, as much as the entheogenic effects of the potion itself, are thought to lead to an "æsthetic frame of mind" considered to be vital to the healing process—music and art as therapy [Gebhart-Sayer 1986]! The lovely tattoos and body paint used by shamans are thought to represent "healthy" versions of the patterns which the shaman can see on the skin of the patient. Different illnesses lead to specific distortions in the healthy designs, and *ayahuasca* is a potent aid for the shaman in "repainting" the patient, thus restoring health[Luna 1992,1993]. Similar æsthetic/therapeutic ideas likely prevailed in ancient Mexican shamanic healing. For the ancient Aztecs, *in xóchitl in cuicatl*— "in flower in song"—was a metaphor for the entheogenic state *temicxoch*, the "flowery dream" of the shaman/priest, expressed in *tecpillatolli*, a sacred language of shamans

[18]

and poets, the divinely-inspired *logos*, oracular speech of the thaumaturge inebriated by entheogenic plants, depicted visually as "speech scrolls" with appended flowers[9] [Cáceres 1984; León Portilla 1961; Ortíz de Montellano 1990]. Naturally such divinely-inspired sound would be thought to have healing properties.

AYAHUASCA ADMIXTURE PLANTS

Although there is some evidence for the use of straight *ayahuasca*—infusions employing *Banisteriopsis caapi* (or a related species) by itself—by far the most common practice is the brewing of potions containing other plants in addition to the *Banisteriopsis* base. These *ayahuasca* additives or admixtures were recently characterized aptly as a "traditional pharmacopœia" [McKenna *et al.* 1986], and indeed, some 97 species in 39 families have been reported as *ayahuasca* additives, many of them are potent entheogens in their own right, and a good many are known sources of biodynamic compounds. The reported *ayahuasca* admixtures are listed in Table I, and several categories of these will be discussed in some detail. Basically, the many *ayahuasca* admixtures may be broken down into three broad categories, each to be discussed in turn: 1) non-psychoactive and presumably therapeutic additives; 2) stimulants; and 3) entheogens or visionary drugs. Since my focus is entheogenic use of *ayahuasca*, the last category will be given by far the greatest attention.

Therapeutic Additives: This is the most nebulous category of *ayahuasca* additives, and is a sort of catch-all to explain, for the nonce, the many non-psychoactive (so far as is known) and pharmacologically-obscure admixture plants, all of which are not likely to be entheogenic. I conjecture that *ayahuasca*, like the ancient Mexican *cacáhuatl* potion based on an aqueous infusion of cacao beans (*Theobroma cacao*), represents a sort of all-purpose pharmacological vehicle. In ancient México, cacao potions were used as a basis for entheogenic *kykeons* containing psilocybian mushrooms and other inebriating plants, as I showed in my book on the subject [Ott 1985]. Such potions were also used for the administration of a great many other medicinal plants with a more specific therapeutic purpose, as even a cursory examination of Francisco Hernández's Mexican plant pharmacopœia will show [Hernández 1651]. I suspect that many of the admixtures to *ayahuasca* must have a specific therapeutic rationale, and are added to *ayahuasca*, the queen of plant medicines, to enhance their efficacy, whether by a specific pharmacological means, or simply by association with the most powerful healing magic known. A recent paper examined the biodynamic ingredients of this "traditional pharmacopœia," concluding that

[19]

many of the plants contained pharmacologically-active constituents (or belonged to genera or families containing such), but whose pharmacological rationale as *ayahuasca* admixtures was a "complete mystery" [McKenna *et al.* 1986]. Even more mysterious were the numerous *ayahuasca* admixtures for which we have no chemical data whatever. I agree with the authors that this category of admixture plants holds great potential interest for western science, and I expect further research will show that some of the unknown plants are psychoactive, while others have more specific therapeutic effects. The fact that Amazonian shamans are known to bioassay unfamiliar plants in self-experiments by adding them to *ayahuasca* [Miller 1993; Montgomery 1992], or by "examining" them while under its influence [Bristol 1966] gives me further confidence in a specific phytotherapeutic dimension of *ayahuasca*. A recent review disclosed that four of the five most common anti-rheumatic plant medicines in Amazonia are known *ayahuasca* additives: *Alchornea castaneifolia*; *Brunfelsia grandiflora* subsp. *schultesii*; *Mansoa alliacea* and *Maytenus ebenifolia* [Prance & Kallunki 1984]. Their use in *ayahuasca* must be therapeutic and non-visionary.

Stimulants: As we will see in Chapters Two and Three, plain infusions of *ayahuasca* have pronounced soporific or sedative effects, and it is therefore not surprising that plants containing known stimulants have been reported as additives to *ayahuasca*, "to give strength to deal with *ayahuasca*" [Schultes & Raffauf 1990]. The most widely reported stimulant additive to *ayahuasca* is *guayusa*, the leaves of *Ilex guayusa* [Shemluck 1979]. The Shuar, Runa and Quijos Quichua Indians of Ecuador add leaves of this traditional stimulant to *ayahuasca* [Furst 1976; Kohn 1992; Ott 1993; Russo 1992; Schultes 1972b; Schultes & Raffauf 1990]. Jesuit missions grew commercial plantations of *guayusa* in the colonial period, and there is a 17th century report of adding *guayusa* to a potion containing *Brugmansia* and *Nicotiana* species, besides *Banisteriopsis* [Schultes 1979b]. *Guayusa* is a close relative of the famous South American stimulant *mate* (or *maté*; *Ilex paraguariensis*, also known scientifically as *I. paraguayensis* or *I. paraguensis*) and of the North American stimulant *yaupon* (*Ilex vomitoria*). Like *I. ambigua*, these species contain caffeine, and leaves of a Shuar strain of *I. guayusa* were recently shown to contain 7.6% caffeine, making this by far the most potent caffeine-containing plant known [Bohinc *et al.* 1977; Lewis *et al.* 1991; Power & Chestnut 1919]. *Yaupon* was reportedly used as an "hallucinogen" to "evoke ecstasies" among North American Cherokee Indians, who, like their Shuar counterparts, used strong infusions of *Ilex* leaves to induce ceremonial vomiting for purification [Hamel & Chiltoskey 1975; Lewis *et al.* 1991].

Similarly, the Amazonian stimulant *yoco* or *Paullinia yoco*, a caffeine-containing relative of the famous Brazilian caffeine-plant *guaraná* (*Paullinia cupana* var. *sorbilis*)

[Henman 1982; Schultes 1942,1986a; Schultes & Raffauf 1992] was recently reported as an *ayahuasca* additive among the Colombian Siona Indians [Langdon 1986]. This important Amazonian stimulant is unique among caffeine-containing drugs in that the bark, rather than the leaves, is the part extracted for its high caffeine content [Schultes 1942,1986a,1987; Schultes & Raffauf 1992]. By the same token, Peruvian Campa and Colombian Barasana Indians may take *ayahuasca* with cocaine-containing leaves of *Erythroxylum coca* var. *ipadú* [Holmstedt *et al.* 1978; Schultes 1981; Wilbert 1987]. In these cases, too, the rationale appears to be a stimulating boost to conteract the soporific affects of *ayahuasca*, and "to give strength to deal with" the drug. As I will describe in Chapter Three, I found the effects of *ayahuasca* prepared using *guayusa* leaves by Quijos Quichua *ayahuasqueros* still to be quite soporific, with no visionary or entheogenic effects.

Entheogens: By far the most interesting category of *ayahuasca* additives are the visionary or entheogenic plants, which fall into four broad subcategories: 1) *Nicotiana* [nicotine]; 2) *Brugmansia* [tropane alkaloids]; 3) *Brunfelsia* [scopoletine]; and 4) *Chacruna/Chagropanga* [DMT], the entheogenic tryptamine-containing plant admixtures. We will briefly discuss these four subgroups, and deal with the last in much greater detail in Chapters Two and Three. All of these plants have the same pharmacological purpose in *ayahuasca*—to enhance the entheogenic/visionary quality of the potions as an aid to shamanic divination. All of the plants in the first three subcategories fall into the family Solanaceae, whereas the tryptamine-containing category involves plants in the families Malpighiaceae and Rubiaceae.

The cultivated tobacco species, *Nicotiana tabacum* and *N. rustica*, are among the most common and widespread of all *ayahuasca* admixture plants. Although this important class of *ayahuasca* additives has been all-but-overlooked in the literature on the potion, Johannes Wilbert recently reviewed the general ethnobotanical literature on tobacco in South America, including its prominence as *ayahuasca* admixture or cohort [Wilbert 1987]. Wilbert mentioned the association of tobacco with *ayahuasca* among the Aguaruna, Barasana, Campa, Cocama, Lamista, Machigenga, Omagua, Piro, Shipibo, Shuar and Tecuana Indians, and such use has also been reported among the Quijos Quichua and Secoya Indians of Ecuador [Ott 1993; Vickers & Plowman 1984]. Sometimes tobacco infusions are added to *ayahuasca*, or drunk alternately with the potion, and at times tobacco accompanies *ayahuasca* in the form of snuffs and clysters, or by smoking [Wilbert 1987]. Tobacco, even more than *ayahuasca*, is *the* shamanic drug of Amazonia and the Americas as a whole—as Wilbert commented of the Záparo Indians, the shamans: "take *ayahuasca*... to see better but believe that their true power derives from tobacco"

[Wilbert 1987,1991]. Tobacco, like *ayahuasca*, is a fundamental "plant teacher" of the aspiring shaman [Schultes & Raffauf 1992] and among the Quijos Quichua, for example, the neophyte shaman must first serve an apprenticeship with tobacco before graduating to an apprenticeship with *ayahuasca* [Alarcón 1990]. Source of the potent psychotropic drug nicotine, which can only enhance the visionary potency of *ayahuasca* potions, South American tobacco species have also been used as dart-poison ingredients [Bisset 1992].

Another important category of visionary additives to *ayahuasca* potions are the entheogenic species of *Brugmansia*, known variously as *huanto, maikoa, misha, etc.* in various Indian languages, and as *borrachero* or *floripondio* in Spanish. The Sharanahua, Shuar, Ingano, Quichua and Siona Indians add *Brugmansia suaveolens* leaves to their *ayahuasca* potions, and leaves of *B. insignis* may also be so used, together with leaves, stems, seeds, and ashes of leaves of other *Brugmansia* species [Chango *et al.* 1984; Langdon 1986; Lockwood 1979; Schultes & Raffauf 1990,1992; Vickers & Plowman 1984]. All of the *Brugmansia* species are potent entheogens in their own right, commonly used as divinatory agents from México [Lipp 1990,1991] south, particularly in the Andes from Colombia to Chile [Polia & Bianchi 1993; Schultes & Raffauf 1990,1992; Walton 1970] and their addition to *ayahuasca* can only result in considerably enhanced visionary potency. We know nothing about the pharmacological interactions of their contained tropane alkaloids, especially scopolamine or hyoscine and hyoscyamine [Bristol *et al.* 1969; El Imam & Evans 1990; Evans *et al.* 1965; Rivera *et al.* 1989], with *ayahuasca*-derived β-carbolines.

The solanaceous *Brunfelsia* species constitute an important, but obscure, category of *ayahuasca* admixture plants. Several Indian groups of Colombia and of Ecuador add bark, leaves or roots of *Brunfelsia grandiflora, B. grandiflora* subsp. *schultesii* or leaves of *B. chiricaspi* to their *ayahuasca* [Kohn 1992; Langdon 1986; Plowman 1977; Schultes & Raffauf 1990,1992]. *Brunfelsia grandiflora* subsp. *schultesii,* known as *chiriguayusa* or *chiric-sananho,* is primarily used in *ayahuasca,* but *chiricaspi,* the *Brunfelsia* species with the same name, is sometimes used as a solitary entheogen by Kofán, Mai Huna, Siona and Ingano Indians [Plowman 1977; Schultes & Raffauf 1990,1992], and is considered to be preferable to *chiriguayusa.* The chemistry of this genus is obscure, but the apparently psychoactive coumarin scopoletine[10] is known from these species, and also from the well-known Brazilian ethnomedicine *manacá,* the root of *Brunfelsia uniflora,* likewise used as a shamanic inebriant [Mors & Ribeiro 1957; Plowman 1977; Schultes & Hofmann 1980].

Of the miscellaneous and chemically obscure admixture plants, a few might be cited as prospective entheogens. The Sharanahua Indians add unidentified species of *Epiphyllum* and *Opuntia* cacti to their *ayahuasca*, the latter making "the effects very strong" [Rivier & Lindgren 1972; Schultes & Raffauf 1990]. Since several species of *Opuntia* are known to contain trace amounts of mescaline, the active entheogen of the famous *péyotl* cactus of México and the United States [Anderson 1980; Ma *et al.* 1986; Ott 1993; Pardanani *et al.* 1978; Schultes & Hofmann 1980], there is the possibility these *ayahuasca* additives may contain the famous entheogen. *Alchornea castaneifolia* was reported as a Peruvian additive [Luna 1984a,1984b] and, since the related species *A. floribunda* is an adjunct to African entheogenic powders based on *eboka, Tabernanthe iboga* [Schultes & Hofmann 1980], both of these euphorbiaceous species must be regarded as probable entheogens. Finally, the use of the myristicaceous *Virola surinamensis* as an *ayahuasca* admixture may suggest the presence of the entheogenic tryptamines found in 13 species of this genus [Holmstedt *et al.* 1980; McKenna *et al.* 1984b]. Indeed, this species is used in the elaboration of entheogenic "pellets" by Bora, Muiname and Witoto Indians of the Colombian Amazon [Schultes 1969b; Schultes & Raffauf 1990,1992; Schultes & Swain 1976; Schultes *et al.* 1977], although preliminary analyses of bark, leaves, seeds and a "paste" of *V. surinamensis* were negative for tryptamines [Holmstedt *et al.* 1980].

Which brings us to the most important category of *ayahuasca* admixture plants, those containing the short-acting entheogenic tryptamines, especially *N,N*-dimethyltryptamine or DMT, and secondarily 5-methoxy-*N,N*-dimethyltryptamine (5-MeO-DMT; present in trace amounts in traditional *ayahuasca* additives but in significant amounts in some prospective *ayahuasca* analogue plants). The most common of these are *chacruna* or *amirucapanga, Psychotria viridis* in the Rubiaceae or coffee family, and *chagropanga, chalipanga* or *oco-yajé, Diplopterys cabrerana* in the same family as *ayahuasca*, Malpighiaceae (previously known in the literature as *Banisteriopsis rusbyana*). In both cases, it is the leaves of these plants which are added to *ayahuasca* to "heighten and lengthen" (if not entirely create) its entheogenic effects [Schultes & Hofmann 1980].

In 1965 José Cuatrecasas reported the collection in the Colombian Putumayo region of an additive to *ayahuasca* in the Malpighiaceae family of *Banisteriopsis caapi*, which Kofán and Inga Indians called *oco-yagé, yagé-úco* or *chagropanga,* and which he called *Banisteriopsis rusbyana* [Cuatrecasas 1965]. Schultes had previously documented the use of the *leaves* of this liana as an *ayahuasca* admixture by Colombian Mocoa Indians [Schultes 1957], and there were additional mentions of it, always referring to the use of leaves and young shoots of the plant [Harner 1973b; Reichel-Dolmatoff 1972,1975]. As cited above, today the plant has been transferred to another genus, and the accepted name is *Diplopterys cabrerana* [Gates 1982,1986].

[23]

In 1965–1968, three different groups reported the isolation [Poisson 1965] or detection [Agurell *et al.* 1968; Der Marderosian *et al.* 1968] of DMT in leaves of *D. cabrerana*. The isolation by Jacques Poisson was from leaves of the plant collected by Claudine Friedberg from Shuar Indians preparing *natema*, and the subsequent detection work involved leaves collected by Homer V. Pinkley, who had observed their use by Kofán Indians of Amazonian Ecuador in the preparation of *ayahuasca*. The fact that it is the *leaves* of this liana, not the bark, that are used in the potions, combined with the fact that these leaves contain tryptamines rather than the characteristic β-carbolines found in *Banisteriopsis*, justifies the inclusion of this plant in the category of admixtures. As I will discuss at length in Chapter Three, there is a definite synergy between the tryptamines, ordinarily inactive orally, and the β-carbolines, which by themselves lack interesting effects.

Like *Banisteriopsis caapi, Diplopterys cabrerana* grows in Amazonian lowlands, and the plant has been collected only in southern Colombia and Venezuela, eastern Ecuador, northern Perú and western Brazil [Gates 1982]. Like *B. caapi, D. cabrerana* rarely flowers, and is normally cultivated by shamans for use in *ayahuasca*. Both plants are commonly propagated by cuttings. While *B. caapi* fruits are triple-winged samaras clearly adapted for aerial dispersal, *D. cabrerana* fruits appear to be adapted for flotation and subsequent water dispersal, leading Gates [1982] to conclude that the natural habitat of the species was riverine (*oco-yajé* in Tukanoan means "water *yajé*"). Collections from Perú and Ecuador were all sterile, suggesting they are cultivars; the only fertile collections were from riverbanks in Brazil, Venezuela and Colombia. Schultes reported that another related species, *Diplopterys involuta* (excluded by Gates from the genus, classified rather as *Mezia includens*) is known as *ayahuasca negro*, suggesting use in the potions, though none has been reported [Schultes 1983]. The ethnobotanical literature is unfortunately vague as to the quantity of leaves of *Diplopterys* which may be added to a typical dose of *ayahuasca*.

Comparatively more is known about the ethnobotany of another foliar additive to *ayahuasca* potions, the leaves of *Psychotria viridis*, in the Rubiaceae or the coffee family. Called *chacruna* in Perú, and *sami ruca* or *amirucapanga* in Ecuador, leaves of this shrub are similarly added to *ayahuasca* to enhance its visionary potency [Kensinger 1973; Kohn 1992; Miller 1993; Prance 1970; Prance & Prance 1970; Prance *et al.* 1977; Schultes 1969b; Weiss 1973]. As was the case with leaves of *Diplopterys cabrerana*, leaves of *Psychotria viridis* contain DMT as principal alkaloid [Der Marderosian *et al.* 1970; Rivier & Lindgren 1972] Again, we will leave until Chapter Three a discussion of the pharmacological synergy between DMT and the *Banisteriopsis* alkaloids; suffice to say that DMT is the key ingredient, responsible for the entheogenic effects of *Diplopterys* or *Psychotria* leaf-containing *ayahuasca* potions—according to Peruvian Indian informants, "one sees nothing" without this ingredient [Rivier & Lindgen 1972]. I would agree with this, modifying it to say one sees nothing *interesting* taking *ayahuasca* without a tryptamine-rich additive, or the addition of some other potent entheogen.

Psychotria carthaginensis has also been reportedly used as an *ayahuasca* admixture, and preliminary studies likewise detected DMT in leaves of this species [Rivier & Lindgren 1972]. Although *Psychotria psychotriaefolia* has been cited in various reports as an *ayahuasca* admixture [Pinkley 1969; Schultes 1969a,1969b], and was even reported to contain DMT [Der Marderosian *et al.* 1970], Schultes since characterized this as an herbarium error [Schultes 1986b], and the material analyzed was actually *P. viridis* [Der Marderosian *et al.* 1970]. Various unidentified species of *Psychotria* are also used as *ayahuasca* admixtures by Peruvian Sharanahua and Cashinahua Indians. *Psychotria* leaves called *pishikawa* and *batsikawa* were added to *ayahuasca* by Sharanahua of the upper Río Purús region [Rivier & Lindgren 1972], and the latter was said to be inferior. This must correspond to the Cashinahua *Psychotria* leaf admixture *matsi kawa*, which was found to be devoid of alkaloids, in contrast to another *Psychotria* leaf additive to *nixi pae* (*ayahuasca*) potions, *nai kawa*, which contained substantial amounts [Der Marderosian *et al.* 1970]. The Cashinahua who prepared the *nixi pae* lived on the Río Curanja, in the same upper Río Purús region of Perú. *Nai kawa* was thought to be *P. alba*, *P. carthaginensis*, *P. horizontalis* or *P. marginata*. Clearly, more detailed taxonomic and ethnobotanical studies are needed to clarify the identity of these *Psychotria* species. A number of species of the genus are used ethnomedicinally throughout Amazonia [Schultes & Raffauf 1990], and *P. insularum* and other species are used widely in Polynesian ethnomedicine [Cox 1991; Whistler 1992].

Psychotria viridis is a shrub or small tree with shiny leaves, somewhat similar in appearance to a coffee tree. The plant is also found in the Amazon lowlands, but grows farther north as well, in Central America, and may also be found in Cuba [Schultes & Hofmann 1980]. Although it produces coffee-bean like seeds, these are difficult to germinate, often taking as much as six months. The plant is easily propagated from leaf cuttings, which are partially buried with the petiole— sometimes fallen leaves spontaneously form daughter plants [Harrison 1993].

This is the overall picture of *ayahuasca* admixture plants—further information can be obtained by consulting the references in Table I. The review by McKenna *et al.* [1986] furnishes chemical and pharmacological details, and see my *Pharmacotheon* for a review of the ethnomedicine of *ayahuasca* additives [Ott 1993]. I might

[25]

mention that some groups are reported to have used various *ayahuasca* additives, such as the Shuar, who have been reported to employ four different entheogenic additives to *natema* or *ayahuasca*—*Diplopterys cabrerana* [Harner 1973b]; *Brunfelsia* species [Schultes & Hofmann 1980]; *Nicotiana* species and *maikoa* or *Brugmansia* species [Schultes & Raffauf 1990]. The Sharanahua of Perú have been cited as using at least nine admixture plants, including the known entheogens *Brugmansia suaveolens* [Schultes & Raffauf 1990] and *Psychotria viridis*, as well as the unidentified *Psychotria* species listed above, and various plants unknown from a chemical/pharmacological perspective [Rivier & Lindgren 1972]. Six prospective additive plants—*Brugmansia versicolor, Ocimum micranthum, Alternanthera* sp., *Cyperus* sp., *Calathea* sp. and *Psychotria poeppigiana*—are reportedly cultivated in home gardens in Peruvian Amazonia, conceivably as *ayahuasca* admixtures [Padoch & De Jong 1991].

While there do exist some reports of taking *ayahuasca* neat, that is, with no ingredients other than *Banisteriopsis* species (such as Spruce's report of Guahibo Indians simply chewing the dried stems of *Banisteriopsis*), we have no information on the resulting effects. In all events, by far the most common practice is brewing potions with one or several additives. We also have little or no information on the effects of tobacco and other solanaceous plants when added to *ayahuasca*, most ethnographers lacking a stomach for "nauseous beverages" like *ayahuasca*. By far the most important additives are the tryptamine-containing leaves. The pharmacognostical evidence we are about to examine will explain why. Plain *ayahuasca* is more of a sedative than a stimulant, and generally speaking, entheogens are stimulants. *Passiflora* species used ethnomedicinally, which also contain *ayahuasca*-type β-carboline alkaloids, are used as sedatives and tranquilizers [Joyal 1987; Monardes 1990; Nicholson & Arzeni 1993; Oga *et al.* 1984; Speroni & Minghetti 1988]. Since our interest here is *ayahuasca* as entheogen, we will focus on the most common additives, the tryptamine-containing *Psychotria* and *Diplopterys* leaves, which in fact are the stimulating and entheogenic constituents of the leaf-enriched *ayahuasca* potions. As we will see, there is a clear-cut pharmacological synergy, which I have been at pains to elucidate *via* self-experiments, between the β-carbolines of *Banisteriopsis* species and the DMT contained in *Psychotria* and *Diplopterys* admixture plants. Indeed, the β-carbolines function here not as specific psychotropic constituents but as enzyme inhibitors, to prevent our bodies from deactivating the DMT contained in the leaves, which is not ordinarily active orally. The sound and the fury in *ayahuasca*, which has attracted so much attention to this pan-Amazonian ambrosia, is ironically a result of alkaloids not found in *Banisteriopsis* species, but extracted from the leaves commonly added to the potions throughout Amazonia!

[26]

TABLE I
AYAHUASCA ADDITIVE PLANTS*

ACANTHACEAE
Teliostachya lanceolata Nees var. *crispa* Nees[1] [Schultes 1972a]
AMARANTHACEAE
Alternanthera lehmannii Hieronymus[1] [García Barriga 1958; Schultes 1957]
Iresine sp. [Schultes & Hofmann 1979] ·
APOCYNACEAE
Himatanthus sucuuba (Spruce ex Mueller-Argoviensis) Woodson [Luna 1984b]
Malouetia tamaquarina (Aublet) DC. [Pinkley 1969; Schultes 1957,1960]
Mandevilla scabra Schumann [Luna & Amaringo 1991]
Tabernaemontana sp. [Luna 1984a,1984b; Pinkley 1969; Schultes 1972a]
AQUIFOLIACEAE
Ilex guayusa Loesner[2] [Furst 1976; Schultes 1972b; Schultes & Raffauf 1990]
ARACEAE
Montrichardia arborescens Schott [Luna 1984a]
BIGNONIACEAE
Mansoa alliacea (Lamarck) A. Gentry[3] [Luna 1984b]
Tabebuia heteropoda (DC.) Sandwith [McKenna *et al.* 1986]
Tabebuia incana A. Gentry [Luna 1984a]
Tabebuia sp. [Luna 1984b]
Tynnanthus panurensis (Burman) Sandwith [Luna 1984b]
BOMBACACEAE
Cavanillesia hylogeiton Ulbrich [Luna & Amaringo 1991]
Cavanillesia umbellata Ruíz et Pavón [Luna & Amaringo 1991]
Ceiba pentandra (L.) Gaertner [Luna 1984b]
Chorisia insignis Humboldt, Bonpland et Kunth [Luna 1984b]
Chorisia speciosa [McKenna *et al.* 1986]
Quararibea "ishpingo" [Arévalo Valera 1986; Wassén 1979]
BORAGINACEAE
Tournefortia angustifolia Roemer et Schultes [Vickers & Plowman 1984]
CACTACEAE
Epiphyllum sp. [Pinkley 1969; Rivier & Lindgren 1972]
Opuntia sp.[1] [Rivier & Lindgren 1972]
CARYOCARACEAE
Anthodiscus pilosus Ducke [McKenna *et al.* 1986]

[27]

CELASTRACEAE
Maytenus ebenifolia Reiss[3] [Luna 1984a,1984b]
CYCLANTHACEAE
Carludovica divergens Ducke [Luna 1984a]
CYPERACEAE
Cyperus digitatus Roxburgh [McKenna *et al.* 1986]
Cyperus prolixus Humboldt, Bonpland et Kunth [McKenna *et al.* 1986]
Cyperus sp. [Pinkley 1969; Rivier & Lindgren 1972]
DRYOPTERIDACEAE
Lomariopsis japurensis (Martius) J. Sm. [Pinkley 1969; Rivier & Lindgren 1972]
ERYTHROXYLACEAE
Erythroxylum coca Lamarck var. *ipadú* Plowman[2] [Wilbert 1987]
EUPHORBIACEAE
Alchornea castaneifolia (Willdenow) Just.[3] [Luna 1984a,1984b]
Hura crepitans L. [Luna 1984a,1984b]
GNETACEAE
Gnetum nodiflorum Brongniart [Schultes & Raffauf 1990]
GUTTIFERAE
Clusia sp. [Rivier & Lindgren 1972; Schultes & Raffauf 1990]
Tovomita sp. [Luna 1984b]
LABIATAE
Ocimum micranthum Willdenow [Pinkley 1969]
LECYTHIDACEAE
Couroupita guianensis Aublet [Luna 1984a,1984b]
LEGUMINOSAE
Bauhinia guianensis Aublet [Luna & Amaringo 1991]
Caesalpinia echinata Lamarck [Luna 1984a]
Calliandra angustifolia Spruce ex Bentham[4] [Luna 1984b]
Campsiandra laurifolia Bentham [Luna 1984a]
Cedrelinga castaneiformis Ducke [Luna 1984b]
Erythrina glauca Willdenow [Luna 1984b]
Erythrina poeppigiana (Walpers) Cook [McKenna *et al.* 1986]
Pithecellobium laetum Bentham [Luna 1984b]
Sclerobium setiferum Ducke [McKenna *et al.* 1986]
Vouacapoua americana Aublet [Luna 1984b]
LORANTHACEAE
Phrygilanthus eugenioides (L.) HBK [Pinkley 1969; Rivier & Lindgren 1972]

Phrygilanthus eugenioides (L.) HBK var. *robustus* Glaz. [McKenna *et al.* 1986]
Phtirusa pyrifolia (HBK) Eichler [Luna 1984a,1984b]
    MALPIGHIACEAE
Diplopterys cabrerana (Cuatrecasas) Gates[1] [Agurell *et al.* 1968; Der Marderosian *et al.* 1968; Pinkley 1969; Poisson 1965; Schultes 1972a]
Diplopterys involuta (Turczaninow) Niedenzu = *Mezia includens* (Bentham) Cuatrecasas[5] [Schultes 1983]
Mascagnia psilophylla (Jussieu) Grisebach var. *antifebrilis* Niedenzu[1] = *Cabi paraensis* (Jussieu) Grisebach; *Callaeum antifebrile* (Grisebach) Johnson [Schultes 1957]
Stigmaphyllon fulgens (Lamarck) Jussieu [Schultes & Raffauf 1990]
    MARANTACEAE
Calathea veitchiana Veitch ex Hooker *fil.* [Schultes 1972a]
    MENISPERMACEAE
Abuta grandifolia (Martius) Sandwith [Luna 1984b]
    MORACEAE
Coussapoa tessmannii Mildbread [McKenna *et al.* 1986]
Ficus insipida Willdenow [Luna 1984b]
Ficus ruiziana Standley [McKenna *et al.* 1986]
Ficus sp. [Luna 1984b]
    MYRISTICACEAE
Virola sp. [Luna 1984b]
Virola surinamensis (Roland) Warburg [Luna 1984a,1984b]
    NYMPHIACEAE
Cabomba aquatica Aublet [McKenna *et al.* 1986]
    PHYTOLACCACEAE
Petiveria alliacea L. [Luna 1984b]
    PIPERACEAE
Piper sp. [Schultes & Raffauf 1990]
    POLYGONACEAE
Triplaris surinamensis Chamisso [Luna 1984a,1984b]
Triplaris surinamensis Cham. var. *chamissoana* Meissner [McKenna *et al.* 1986]
    PONTEDERIACEAE
Pontederia cordata L.[5] [Schultes 1972a]
    RUBIACEAE
Calycophyllum spruceanum (Bentham) Hooker *fil.* ex Schumann [Luna 1984a]
Capirona decorticans Spruce [Luna 1984b]

[29]

RUBIACEAE
Guettarda ferox Standley [McKenna *et al.* 1986]
Psychotria carthaginensis Jacquin[1] [Luna 1984a; Pinkley 1969; Schultes 1972a]
Psychotria psychotriaefolia (Seemann) Standley [Pinkley 1969; Prance 1970]
Psychotria "batsikawa" [Der Marderosian *et al.* 1970; Rivier & Lindgren 1972]
Psychotria "nai kawa" [Der Marderosian *et al.* 1970]
Psychotria "pishikawa" [Rivier & Lindgren 1972]
Psychotria viridis Ruíz et Pavón[1] [Luna 1984a; Pinkley 1969; Prance 1970]
Rudgea retifolia Standley [Schultes 1985a; Schultes & Raffauf 1990]
Sabicea amazonensis Wernham [Hugh-Jones 1979; Schultes 1985a; Schultes &
    Raffauf 1990,1992]
Uncaria guianensis (Aublet) Gmelin [McKenna *et al.* 1986]
    SAPINDACEAE
Paullinia yoco Schultes et Killip[2] [Langdon 1986]
    SCHIZAEACEAE
Lygodium venustum Swartz [Pinkley 1969; Rivier & Lindgren 1972]
    SCROPHULARIACEAE
Scoparia dulcis L. [Luna 1984b]
    SOLANACEAE
Brugmansia insignis (Barbosa-Rodrígues) Lockwood ex Schultes[1] [Schultes &
    Raffauf 1990]
Brugmansia suaveolens (Humboldt et Bonpland ex Willdenow) Berchtold et Presl[1]
    [Dobkin de Ríos 1970b; Luna 1984a,1984b; Rivier & Lindgren 1972]
Brunfelsia chiricaspi Plowman[1] [Plowman 1977]
Brunfelsia grandiflora D. Don[1] [Plowman 1977; Schultes & Raffauf 1990]
Brunfelsia grandiflora D. Don subsp. *schultesii* Plowman[1,3] [Luna 1984b; Pinkley
    1969; Plowman 1977; Schultes & Raffauf 1990]
Capsicum sp. [Rivier & Lindgren 1972; Schultes & Raffauf 1990]
Iochroma fuchsioides (HBK) Miers[1] [McKenna *et al.* 1986; Schultes 1977]
Juanulloa ochracea Cuatrecasas[5] [Schultes 1972a]
Nicotiana rustica L.[1] [Luna 1984b; Wilbert 1987]
Nicotiana tabacum L.[1] [Luna 1984b; Schultes 1972a; Wilbert 1987]
    VERBENACEAE
Cornutia odorata (Poeppig et Endlicher) Poeppig [McKenna *et al.* 1984a]
Vitex triflora Vahl [McKenna *et al.* 1986]
    VIOLACEAE
Rinorea viridiflora Rusby[5] [Schultes & Raffauf 1990]

[30]

NOTES

[1] These *ayahuasca* additives are known entheogenic plants, many of which are at times used alone for their entheogenic effect, in absence of *ayahuasca*.

[2] These *ayahuasca* cohorts are known stimulants, used alone and as *ayahuasca* additives. In the latter case, their function appears to be counteracting the marked soporific effects of *ayahuasca*, so shaman or patient will not fall asleep during the session. Both *Ilex guayusa* and *Paullinia yoco* are known to be abundant sources of the stimulant caffeine [Lewis *et al.* 1991; Schultes 1986a; Schultes & Raffauf 1990], and *Erythroxlum coca* var. *ipadú* is a known source of the stimulant cocaine [Holmstedt *et al.* 1971; Plowman 1981].

[3] These four species were recently reported as among the five principal anti-rheumatic phytomedicines of Amazonia [Prance & Kallunki 1984]. Their use in *ayahuasca* may be related to this specific therapeutic indication.

[4] I was told by a Shuar *ayahuasquero* that *Calliandra* bark is used interchangeably with tryptamine-rich leaves as an *ayahuasca* admixture, proportioning identical effects. This suggests *Calliandra* bark may be a source of DMT. Root infusions of *C. angustifolia* are used as a stimulant by Colombian Indians of the Río Pastaza area [Schultes & Raffauf 1990].

[5] These species have not been reported used as *ayahuasca* additives, but are presumed to have been, because they are sometimes known by the name *ayahuasca* or *chacruna* or are otherwise related to the famous potion [Schultes 1972a, 1985a; Schultes & Raffauf 1990].

[*] This Table lists plant species reportedly used as additives or "admixtures" to entheogenic *ayahuasca* potions in Amazonia. In many cases, the additives are said to "heighten and lengthen" the entheogenic properties of the brews [Schultes & Hofmann 1980]. In other cases, additive plants are stimulants whose effects counteract the soporific properties of the simple extracts of *Banisteriopsis caapi* [Furst 1976; Schultes & Raffauf 1990]. Finally, some additives appear to be therapeutic [Luna 1984a, 1984b; Luna & Amaringo 1991; McKenna *et al.* 1986; Prance & Kallunki 1984] and probably do not exert psychoactive effects. Many of the plants listed here are unknown chemically and the rationale for their use in *ayahuasca* is obscure. Certainly some of these unknown plants will prove to be psychoactive. The chemistry of 56 species of *ayahuasca* additives has recently been reviewed by D.J. McKenna and colleagues, who aptly characterize the Amazonian *ayahuasca* complex as a "traditional pharmacopœia" [McKenna *et al.* 1986]. There may be some duplication in this table. Luna [1984a] reported a *Tabebuia* species as *ayahuasca* additive, then two years later reported *Tabebuia heteropoda* as additive [McKenna *et al.* 1986]. The *Cyperus* species reported as *ayahuasca* admixture two decades ago [Pinkley 1969; Rivier & Lindgren 1972] may be either *C. prolixus* or *C. digitatus* reported subsequently (the former in the English and the latter in the Spanish of McKenna *et al.* 1986). The *Ficus* species that Luna [1984b] reported may be *F. ruiziana* he reported two years later [McKenna *et al.* 1986]. Table was adapted from *Pharmacotheon* [Ott 1993], with minor modifications.

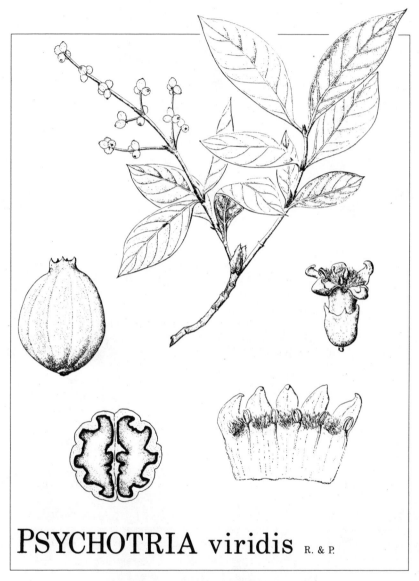

PSYCHOTRIA viridis R. & P.

Above left: Fruit, enlarged 4 times.
Center: Flowering branch; about one-third size.
Right: Flower, magnified some 3 times.
Lower left: Sectioned fruit, enlarged four-fold.
Right: Dissected corolla, enlarged 3 times.

CHAPTER TWO
Pharmacognosy of Ayahuasca
Plants and Potions

The phytochemical study of *ayahuasca* lianas and potions commenced in the first decade of the twentieth century, when in 1905 a Colombian pharmacist, Rafael Zerda Bayón, isolated an amorphous preparation from a *yajé* potion that he called *telepatina* or telepathine [Zerda Bayón 1915]. Eighteen years were to pass before fellow Colombian chemist G. Fischer Cárdenas, in his doctoral thesis, reported the isolation of crystalline material of Zerda Bayón's *telepatina* from plant material of *yajé*, which he believed to be a species of *Aristolochia*, as we saw in the previous chapter [Fischer Cárdenas 1923]. The following year, H. Seil and E. Putt reported the results of a "preliminary" examination of *caapi*, plant material they called *Banisteria caapi*—the isolation of three impure alkaloids [Seil & Putt 1924]. A year later, the Colombian chemist A.M. Barriga Villalba reported the isolation of two alkaloids, *yajéina* and *yajénina* from *yajé* plant matter he'd identified as *Prestonia* [*Haemadictyon*] *amazonica*, also mentioned in another doctoral dissertation published that year in Bogotá, by Colombian chemist L. Albarracín [Albarracín 1925; Barriga Villalba 1925a,1925b].

After this pioneering work in Colombia, the scene shifted to Europe, and in 1926, Europeans E. Clinquart and M. Michiels likewise reported isolation of *yajéine* and *yajénine* from plant samples identified as *Prestonia amazonica* [Clinquart 1926; Michiels & Clinquart 1926]. The situation clarified somewhat the following year, when E. Perrot and Raymond-Hamet reported the equivalence of *télépathine* and *yagéine*, which they isolated from *Banisteria caapi* [Perrot & Raymond-Hamet 1927a,1927b], but was again muddied the following year when famed German chemist Louis Lewin published his isolation of *banisterin* from *yajé* material he had obtained from the Merck company and also called *Banisteria caapi* [Lewin 1928, 1929]. Lewin's colleagues at Merck, K. Rumpf and O. Wolfes, and Swiss chemist F. Elger began to clarify matters considerably, when they reported that Zerda Bay-

[33]

ón's and Fischer Cárdenas' *telepatina*, Barriga Villalba's and Albarracín's *yajéina*, and Lewin's *banisterin* were all equivalent to harmine, a conclusion seconded by three other groups the following year [Brückl & Mussgnug 1929; Dalmer 1929; Elger 1928; Keller & Gottauf 1929; Wolfes & Rumpf 1928]. As though unaware of these advances in distant Europe, a South American thesis from Perú a decade later revived the concepts *yajéina* and *yajénina* for alkaloids isolated from *B. caapi* [Arispe 1938]. All of these studies suffered, however, from a lack of botanical voucher specimens to back up the botanical names associated with this chemical work.

Finally, in 1939, chemists A.L. and K.K. Chen, working with botanical material collected by botanist Llewellyn Williams near Iquitos, Perú and definitively identified as *Banisteriopsis caapi*, showed that telepathine, yajéine and banisterine were in fact identical to harmine [Chen & Chen 1939; Williams 1931]. These researchers were able to isolate harmine from stems, leaves and roots of the documented *B. caapi* sample. Elger had already convincingly established identity of telepathine, yajéine and banisterine with harmine, by comparing crystalline harmine isolated from *Banisteriopsis* with synthetic harmine and harmine he isolated from *Peganum harmala* [Elger 1928]. This well-known alkaloid had been isolated from seeds of Syrian rue, *Peganum harmala*, by German chemist J. Fritzsche midway through the nineteenth century [Fritzsche 1847]. The structure of harmine was also known [Perkin & Robinson 1919a,1919b], and the alkaloid was first synthesized in 1927 [Manske *et al.* 1927; Späth & Lederer 1930a,1930b]. Harmine was found to be 7-methoxy-1-methyl-β-carboline, sharing the β-carboline ring (a tricyclic indole nucleus known technically as pyrido[3,4-*b*]indole) with other alkaloids already known from *Peganum harmala* seeds, such as harmaline [Göbel 1841], harmalol [Fischer 1885; Göbel 1841], harmol, ruine, dihydroruine and leptaflorine or tetrahydroharmine (THH) [Allen & Holmstedt 1980]; some of which, as we will see, were later isolated also from *Banisteriopsis* species. Thus, by 1929 it was definitively demonstrated that the principal alkaloid of *ayahuasca* plants was harmine, a compound of known structure which had already been synthesized.

Chemical studies continued on the *ayahuasca* complex, and the name yajéine was further associated with the drug in two papers appearing in the 1950s [Costa 1956; Mors & Zaltzman 1954]. In one of these papers, yajéine or harmine was also isolated from stems and leaves of a plant then called *Cabi paraensis*, which Gates considered to be identical to *Callaeum antifebrile* (known by synonyms *Banisteria antifebrile* and *Mascagnia psilophylla* var. *antifebrilis*, and definitely used as febrifuge and possibly as an ingredient in *ayahuasca*) [Gates 1982,1986; Mors & Zaltzman 1954]. In 1957, studying botanically-undocumented *Banisteriopsis* material from the Río Napo area, American researchers F.A. Hochstein and A.M. Paradies isolated 0.30% harmine as the major alkaloid, and also reported lesser amounts of harmaline (previously known from *Peganum harmala* seeds) and of *d*-tetrahydroharmine in the dried ground vine [Hochstein & Paradies 1957]. Although *d,l*- or *racemic* tetrahydroharmine (a mixture of two optical or stereoisomers, which are mirror images of an asymmetric molecule differing in that they rotate plane-polarized light in opposite directions, *dextro*-rotatory or *levo*-rotatory, as viewed in a device called a polarimeter; a 50:50 mixture, called a *racemate*, of the two stereoisomers is optically inactive, since this effect or "optical activity" cancels itself out) was already known from *Leptactinia densiflora* in the family Rubiaceae [Paris *et al.* 1955,1957] and from laboratory synthesis, this is the first time the *d*-isomer had been found in nature. Since the racemic compound had already been named leptaflorine, the *ayahuasca d*-tetrahydroharmine is properly designated *d*-leptaflorine, and its absolute configuration was determined to be (+)-1,2,3,4-tetrahydroharmine [Kobilcová & Trojánek 1966]. Hochstein and Paradies also found harmine, harmaline and *d*-leptaflorine (also called THH) in an aqueous extract of *B. caapi* "as used by the natives," and were able to isolate harmine from this. They astutely conjectured that harmaline and *d*-leptaflorine might have "substantial psychotomimetic [*sic*] activity in their own right" [Hochstein & Paradies 1957].

In 1968 another American group studied botanically-documented material of *Banisteriopsis caapi* roots and rhizomes from the Colombian Putumayo region, collected by Richard Evans Schultes. This group found both harmine and harmaline in this material, and also found both compounds in stem material of *B. inebriens* [*sic*] also collected by Schultes, a species now considered to be synonymous with *B. caapi* [Der Marderosian *et al.* 1968; Gates 1982]. The following year, Schultes and colleagues studied chemically the stem material from Richard Spruce's original type collection of *Banisteriopsis caapi*, which the great pioneer had sent to Kew Gardens with his voucher specimen in 1853. Despite various misfortunes which befell the material in transit, it arrived and was preserved in England. Schultes succeeded in procuring five pieces of the material weighing 26.7 g, and at the Karolinska Institutet in Stockholm, the Swedish chemists Bo Holmstedt and Jan-Erik Lindgren finally followed through on Spruce's initiative 115 years later! Using the technique known as GC/MS (gas chromatography/mass spectrometry), they analyzed 11.5 g of Spruce's collection, finding the material to contain 0.40% alkaloids, all harmine [Schultes *et al.* 1969]. They also analyzed a fresh collection of *B. caapi*, finding it to contain 0.50% alkaloids, mainly harmine, with lesser amounts of harmaline and *d*-leptaflorine (THH), plus "two minor components." Thus, after 115 years and the rigors of boat travel from the upper Amazon to England, Spruce's type collection contained amounts of alkaloids comparable to fresh material! It is probable, as we will see later, that the sample had contained the unstable harmaline and *d*-leptaflorine, but that these had decomposed over the years to the more stable harmine. In 1965 a single sample of *Banisteriopsis* stem used in preparation of *natem[a]* by the Shuar Indians had been shown to contain 0.21% harmine and "a minimal quantity of another alkaloid" [Poisson 1965]. Although cited under the concept *B. inebrians*, this material would now be classified as *B. caapi* [Gates 1982].

Yet another American group in 1970 reported analysis of a Cashinahua *nixi pae* (*ayahuasca*) potion prepared during August 1966 on the Río Curanja of Amazonian Perú (see pages 17 and 25 for comments on the preparation of this potion), containing *Banisteriopsis* stems and *Psychotria* leaves. Although the potion had been "kept at room temperature for at least two years" prior to analysis, it was found to contain low but detectable amounts of both harmine and harmaline. Owing to an apparent confusion between harmine and harmaline in the discussion (while the potion was said to contain "much harmaline, and a little harmine" the authors were able to isolate crystalline *harmine* from the potion, suggesting that *harmine* was the major alkaloid; although 0.011% harmaline and 0.007% harmine were reported; that is, roughly 50% more harmaline than harmine), it is difficult to draw quantitative conclusions[11]—the authors stated vaguely that a typical dose of 240 ml contained "about 0.02 g of harmine or harmaline" plus 30 mg DMT [Der Marderosian *et al.* 1970]. We will return to this paper in a discussion of the tryptamine-containing leaf additives to *ayahuasca*.

Two years later, Swiss chemist Laurent Rivier and Swedish chemist Jan-Erik Lindgren published the most complete analytical study of *ayahuasca* plants and potions yet conducted [Rivier & Lindgren 1972]. Working with material used in *ayahuasca* potions mainly by the Sharanahua and Culina Indians of the upper Río Purús of Amazonian Perú (the neighbors of the Cashinahua studied by Der Marderosian's group), these researchers made 30 separate analyses of 16 different *Banisteriopsis* samples,[12] again using GC/MS. Total alkaloid levels in dried stems were from 0.05–0.83% (15 samples); in the branches 0.14–0.37% (4 samples); in leaves 0.25–1.90% (5 samples); in roots 0.61–1.95% (5 samples); with a single sample of seeds containing 0.91% alkaloids. All samples but two contained harmine as the main alkaloid, representing between 40 and 98% of the alkaloidal fraction. In the two exceptions, 42% harmine was exceeded by 47% *d*-leptaflorine in stem material obtained from Piro Indians of Perú, and 40% harmine was surpassed by 44% *d*-leptaflorine in roots of Río Purús *B. caapi*, the stem, branches and leaves of which contained 77–94% of their total alkaloids as harmine. With these two exceptions, all samples contained *d*-leptaflorine as the second most important alkaloid, representing from 1–47% of the alkaloidal fraction, whereas harmaline was the third most concentrated leaf alkaloid, from traces up to 17% of the alkaloidal fraction. Also present were harmol (in eight of the samples, as much as 3%) and 6-methoxytryptamine (in four of the samples, traces except for one sample containing 1%). Rivier and Lindgren also analyzed nine *ayahuasca* potions, some of which they ingested personally. All but two of the potions (one of which contained more DMT than anything else; one of which had *d*-leptaflorine as major alkaloid) contained harmine as the major alkaloid (22–62% of the alkaloidal fraction), with DMT as the second most important alkaloid (20–41%, though three contained none). The second most important β-carboline, present in all samples from 6–40%, was *d*-leptaflorine, with harmaline bringing up the rear, present in all but one, at a level of traces through 4% of the alkaloidal fraction. Rivier & Lindgren concluded that a typical, 200 ml dose of the Río Purús *ayahuasca* contained 65 mg of alkaloids— 25 mg DMT plus 40 mg of β-carbolines as three parts harmine to one part *d*-leptaflorine, with only insignificant traces of harmaline [Rivier & Lindgren 1972].

Another important study of *ayahuasca* plants and potions was done by Dennis J. McKenna's group more than a decade later. The group studied six *Banisteriopsis* samples, mainly from Iquitos and Tarapoto, Perú, and determined total alkaloid concentrations of 0.17–1.36%, finding all but one to contain harmine as the major alkaloid (present at levels of 0.057–0.64% in dried stems). The one exception contained slightly more harmaline, which was found to be the second most important alkaloid in three of the other five samples (present at levels of 0.05–0.38%), while *d*-leptaflorine was the third most important alkaloid (levels of 0.025–0.38%). Low levels of harmol were detected in all samples, and harmalol in two. This group also analyzed quantitatively nine *ayahuasca* potions from the same areas (plus Pucallpa), five undiluted, using high-pressure liquid chromatography (HPLC). Averaging the five samples, McKenna found an alkaloid content of 0.73%, with 65% of the alkaloids as harmine, 22% as *d*-leptaflorine, 6% as harmaline and 8% as DMT. These researchers reported that a typical Pucallpa dose was about 60 ml (range 55–60 ml), which would contain, on average, 437 mg of alkaloids—280 mg harmine, 96 mg *d*-leptaflorine, 25 mg harmaline and 36 mg DMT [McKenna *et al.* 1984a].[13]

The most recent quantitative analysis of *ayahuasca* potions involved a sample of *Santo Daime* (see Chapter Four) from the Brazilian Christian *ayahuasca* cult. While not reporting analysis of source plants (*Banisteriopsis caapi* and *Psychotria viridis*), the European group conducted a GC/MS analysis of a 50 ml dose of the potion, finding it to contain 170.5 mg of alkaloids, with 44% (74.5 mg) of harmine, 41% (69.5 mg) *d*-leptaflorine and 15% (26.5 mg) DMT. Only traces of harmaline were found [Liwszyc *et al.* 1992]. We will return to the foregoing reports in subsequent discussions of *ayahuasca* pharmacology. Traces of six other β-carbolines, which may be artefacts of chemical manipulation [McKenna 1992], have also been found in *Banisteriopsis caapi* [Hashimoto & Kawanishi 1975,1976] as well as the pyrrolidine alkaloids shihunine and dihydroshihunine [Kawanishi *et al.* 1982].

Thus we've quantitative data from five separate studies of 25 samples of *Banisteriopsis caapi* stems (normally used in the potions), with the range of total alkaloid concentration in dried material from 0.05–1.36%, mainly harmine, secondarily *d*-leptaflorine, tertiarily harmaline. Similar alkaloid levels were found in branches and seeds, somewhat higher levels in roots (0.61–1.95%) and in leaves (0.25–1.90%). These data (stem analyses only) are summarized in Table II-A.

TABLE II–A
REPORTED ANALYSES OF *AYAHUASCA* PLANTS (DRIED STEMS)

	Alkaloid Range	Average
Hochstein & Paradies 1957 (1)	—	0.30%
Poisson 1965 (1 sample)	—	0.21%
Schultes *et al.* 1969 (2 samples)	0.40–0.50%	0.45%
Rivier & Lindgren 1972 (15 samples)	0.05–0.83%	0.35%
McKenna *et al.* 1984a (6 samples)	0.17–1.36%	0.78%
Overall Average (all 25 samples)	0.05–1.36%	**0.45%**

Some chemical studies have been conducted on a few *Banisteriopsis* species besides *caapi. Banisteriopsis muricata,* said to be used under the names *míi* and *sacha ayahuasca* by the Waorani and Witoto Indians respectively [Davis & Yost 1983], has been reported (as *Banistereopsis* [*sic*] *argentea*) to contain five β-carbolines in leaves and stems, including harmine and *d*-leptaflorine. Interestingly, DMT was also reported to occur in this species, but alkaloid levels were rather low, 0.02% total. Harmine was the principal alkaloid (0.006%), followed by *d*-leptaflorine (0.005%), 5-methoxy-tetrahydroharman (0.004%), *N*-methyl-tetrahydroharman (0.002%), and lastly harmaline (0.001%). DMT was present at a low level of 0.003%, accompanied by DMT-*N*-oxide at 0.001% [Ghosal 1972; Ghosal & Mazumder 1971; Ghosal *et al.* 1971c]. *Banisteriopsis lutea* was reported to contain harmine [Allen & Holmstedt 1980], but under the synonym *B. nitrosiodora* was said to be "practically devoid of alkaloids" [Deulofeu 1967]. Harmine was also found in the above-mentioned *Callaeum antifebrile* (as *Cabi paraensis*) [De Siqueira-Jaccoud 1959; Mors & Zaltzman 1954]. We have no chemical information on other minor species of *ayahuasca* lianas, although *Banisteria chrysophylla* (=*Heteropterys chrysophylla*, according to Gates) has been reported to contain alkaloids [Gates 1982; Webb 1949]. There is also a report of harmine in the stems of *Banisteriopsis inebrians* [O'Connell & Lynn 1953], which would today be classified as *B. caapi* [Gates 1982].

Let us now examine the chemical studies of the *Diplopterys* and *Psychotria* leaf admixtures to *ayahuasca* potions. In 1965, the French researcher Jacques Poisson, working with leaves of *Diplopterys cabrerana* (reported as *Banisteriopsis rusbyana*) collected by Claudine Friedberg from plants used by Shuar ("Jívaro") Indians in the preparation of *natem[a]* or *ayahuasca*, isolated 0.64% DMT from a small sample of dried leaves [Poisson 1965]. Although Hochstein and Paradies [1957] had reported their isolation of DMT from "an aqueous extract of leaves" used in *ayahuasca* near Iquitos, Perú (and called by them *yage* or *Prestonia amazonica*), this was the first isolation of DMT from identifiable leaves used in actual preparation of an *ayahuasca* potion. In 1968 two independent groups reported their detection of DMT in leaves of *Diplopterys cabrerana*, again cited as *B. rusbyana*. In both cases, the leaf matter was collected by Homer V. Pinkley, who observed its use in preparation of *ayahuasca* by Ecuadorian Kofán Indians in 1966 [Pinkley 1969]. In the first study, chromatographic analysis showed presence of DMT in the leaves, and gas chromatographic quantitation (8 runs) established an approximate concentration of 1.46% DMT in the dried leaves [Der Marderosian *et al.* 1968]. A second gas chromatographic study of the material reported in the same issue of the same journal, found 0.46% DMT in dried leaves, with trace amounts of *N*-methyltryptamine (MMT), 5-methoxy-*N,N*-dimethyltryptamine (or 5-MeO-DMT), 5-hydroxy-*N,N*-dimethyltryptamine (5-OH-DMT or bufotenine) and *N*-methyl-tetrahydro-β-carboline [Agurell *et al.* 1968]. A more recent study of *D. cabrerana* leaves used as *ayahuasca* admixtures in Perú found 0.17% DMT plus "extremely trace amounts" of 5-OH-DMT or bufotenine [McKenna *et al.* 1984a]. In summary, from 0.17–1.75% DMT was reported from *Diplopterys cabrerana* leaves in four separate studies.

The 1970 study of plant ingredients in the Cashinahua *nixi pae* potion of the upper Río Purús area in Perú showed DMT in *Psychotria psychotriaefolia* leaf, later correctly identified as *P. viridis*. This sample was used for comparison purposes—*nixi pae* prepared for the study involved two additional species of *Psychotria*, called *nai kawa* and *matsi kawa*. The latter was found to be devoid of alkaloids, whereas leaves and stems of the former (thought to be either *P. alba*, *P. carthaginensis*, *P. hor-*

[39]

izontalis or *P. marginata*) contained from 0.16–0.22% DMT and lesser amounts of dehydro-DMT, thought to be an artefact of the analysis [Der Marderosian *et al.* 1970]. Rivier and Lindgren analyzed two *P. viridis* samples, finding one to contain 0.34% alkaloids in dried leaves, of which 99% was DMT with traces of MMT and 2-methyl-tetrahydro-β-carboline (MTHC); whereas the second contained merely 0.11% alkaloids, with no DMT and 85% MMT plus 12% MTHC. One sample of *P. carthaginensis* contained 0.66% alkaloids in dried leaves, which was 99% DMT, with traces of the other two compounds. *Psychotria bacteriophylla, P. emetica, P. undulata* and an unidentified *Psychotria* species were all devoid of alkaloids [Rivier & Lindgren 1972]. A more recent analysis of three samples of *P. viridis* used as *ayahuasca* admixtures in Perú found 0.10–0.16% DMT in all samples, with no other alkaloids save traces of MTHC in one. A single *P. carthaginensis* sample was found to be devoid of alkaloids [McKenna *et al.* 1984a]. Thus three separate studies have found from 0–0.66% DMT in *Psychotria* leaves used as *ayahuasca* additives. These data on the quantitative analysis of DMT in the leaf admixtures to *ayahuasca* are summarized in Table II-B, both for *D. cabrerana* and various species of *Psychotria*.

TABLE II–B
REPORTED ANALYSES OF *AYAHUASCA* LEAF ADMIXTURES

	DMT Range	Average
Diplopterys cabrerana		
Poisson 1965 (1 sample)	—	0.64%
Der Marderosian *et al.* 1968 (1)	1.33–1.75%	1.46%
Agurell *et al.* 1968 (1 sample)	—	0.46%
McKenna *et al.* 1984a (1 sample)	—	0.17%
Overall Average (all 4 samples)	0.17–1.75%	**0.68%**
Psychotria species (*P. viridis, P. carthaginensis, nai kawa*)		
Der Marderosian *et al.* 1970 (4)	0.16–0.22%	0.19%
Rivier & Lindgren 1972 (3)	0.00–0.66%	0.33%
McKenna *et al.* 1984a (4)	0.00–0.16%	0.10%
Overall Average (all 11 samples)	0.00–0.66%	**0.20%**

The limited quantitative data we have from four separate analyses of 16 samples of Peruvian and Brazilian *ayahuasca* potions are summarized in Table II-C. The most complete analysis, of nine potions prepared by Sharanahua and Culina Indians of the upper Río Purús had found an average of 40 mg β-carbolines and 25 mg DMT *per* typical, 200 ml dose [Rivier & Lindgren 1972]. Analysis of the single potion prepared by neighboring Cashinahua Indians had found similar amounts of DMT in a typical 240 ml dose, 30 mg, but only 20 mg of β-carbolines *per* dose were found [Der Marderosian *et al.* 1970]. We must recall that this sample had been kept a minimum of two years without refrigeration prior to analysis, and undoubtedly some of the β-carbolines had decomposed. In the McKenna group's average of five samples of *ayahuasca* from the Iquitos and Tarapoto area of Perú, a typical dose of 60 ml contained 401 mg of β-carbolines and 36 mg DMT, and the single analysis of *Santo Daime* from Brazil found a 50 ml dose to contain 144 mg β-carbolines and 26.5 mg of DMT [Liwszyc *et al.* 1992; McKenna *et al.* 1984a]. The overall average for all of the 16 samples analyzed is 158 mg β-carbolines and 29 mg DMT *per* dose.

TABLE II–C
REPORTED ANALYSES OF *AYAHUASCA* POTIONS (AVERAGE *PER* DOSE)

	β-Carbolines	DMT
Der Marderosian *et al.* 1970 (1)	20 mg	30 mg
Rivier & Lindgren 1972 (9)	40 mg	25 mg
McKenna *et al.* 1984a (5 samples)	401 mg	36 mg
Liwszyc *et al.* 1992 (1, *Santo Daime*)	144 mg	26 mg
Overall Average (all 16 samples)	**158 mg**	**29 mg**

All these samples were prepared with *Psychotria* leaf admixtures, and the contents of DMT *per* dose are quite consistent (25, 26.5, 30, 36 mg), but how do we explain the great variation in β-carboline levels, from 40 mg (if we exclude as unreliable the data from the aged Cashinahua potion) to 401 mg *per* dose, an order of magnitude difference? We mustn't forget that in the Río Purús area, where the lower levels were found, the *ayahuasca* is only heated for about one hour, whereas in the Pucallpa area 10–15 hour cooking times are typical, and the brew is concentrated before ingestion. In the Río Purús area, doses of 200–240 ml are typical, whereas near Iquitos, doses of the concentrated potion were in the range of 55–60 ml, and a dose "rarely exceeds 75 ml" [McKenna *et al.* 1984a]. Differences in cooking time could explain much of the discrepancy, and we must also recall the indigenous belief in distinct "kinds" of *Banisteriopsis caapi*, which seem to represent clones of chemical races [Schultes 1986a]. Indeed, the two *ayahuasca* clones analyzed by Rivier and Lindgren from the Iquitos (0.57% alkaloids) and Tarapoto (0.83%) area of Perú contained much higher levels of alkaloids than did the seven clones analyzed from the upper

Río Purús area (0.11, 0.11, 0.20, 0.20, 0.20, 0.21, 0.41%) which had yielded potions with the lower amounts of β-carbolines *per* dose (McKenna's two Iquitos clones averaged 0.52% alkaloids; his two Tarapoto clones 0.51%). We must also take into consideration factors such as varying amounts of plant material being added to the potions, and imprecision as far as gauging doses is concerned. The practice of taking several doses during a single session in some areas may also be important, as many anthropological reports mention supplementary doses of *ayahuasca*.

Chemical differences between the source plant composition and composition of the potions are also worthy of comment. Whereas we have seen that McKenna's group found harmaline as the major alkaloid in one of six *B. caapi* cultivars studied, and to be more concentrated than *d*-leptaflorine in three others, with a fourth containing equivalent amounts of both compounds; three studies of *ayahuasca* potions have found only traces of harmaline in two cases [Liwszyc *et al.* 1992; Rivier & Lindgren 1972] with insignificant amounts in the third [McKenna *et al.* 1984a]. We must also recall that the analysis of Spruce's type specimen of *B. caapi* 115 years after collection showed β-carboline amounts similar to fresh material, but all as harmine, with no harmaline or *d*-leptaflorine [Schultes *et al.* 1969]. It is known that harmaline can be chemically oxidized to harmine in acidic conditions [Iyer & Robinson 1934] or chemically reduced to leptaflorine in alkaline conditions [Perkin & Robinson 1919a]. Evidently the prolonged storage, in the case of Spruce's type material, and the prolonged heating, in the case of well-cooked *ayahuasca*, causes destruction of harmaline, although harmine and/or leptaflorine are possible degradation products. Structures of major *ayahuasca* alkaloids are shown in Table II-D. Harmaline might also be called 3,4-dihydroharmine; leptaflorine called 1,2-dihydroharmaline or 1,2,3,4-tetrahydroharmine (commonly abbreviated THH).[14]

PSYCHOPHARMACOLOGY OF β-CARBOLINES

Although harmine and harmaline had been discovered in the 1840s, the context of the research was a study of pigments, not of drugs, and it wasn't until the isolation of harmine from *Banisteriopsis caapi* that pharmacological studies of the alkaloid were initiated. The famed mescaline researcher Alexandre Rouhier conducted some early research on yajéine (harmine) in animals [Rouhier 1924, 1926], but it was Louis Lewin, like Rouhier best known for his work on *péyotl* [Lewin 1888; Rouhier 1927], who first tested the drug on human beings. Lewin reported that 25–75 mg of harmine injected subcutaneously provoked euphoria in human subjects [Lewin

1928]. Lewin and Paul Schuster tested harmine (banisterine) as a therapy for Parkinsonism, injecting 20–40 mg doses into 18 patients, evoking some transient improvement [Lewin & Schuster 1929]. Just before his death, Lewin published a brief monograph on *Banisteria caapi: Ein Neues Rauschgift und Heilmittel* (*Banisteria caapi: A New Narcotic and Medicament*) [Lewin 1929]. Another German scientist who is today best-known for his studies of *péyotl*/mescaline, Kurt Beringer [1927], working with K. Wilmanns, had further researched "banisterine" as a therapy in Parkinsonism, giving patients 20 mg doses four to six times daily [Beringer 1928; Beringer & Wilmanns 1929]. Beringer remarked on the similarity between harmine and banisterine pharmacology, just as the chemical equivalence of the two was being established by his German scientific colleagues [Beringer 1929].

TABLE II–D
STRUCTURES OF MAJOR *AYAHUASCA* ALKALOIDS

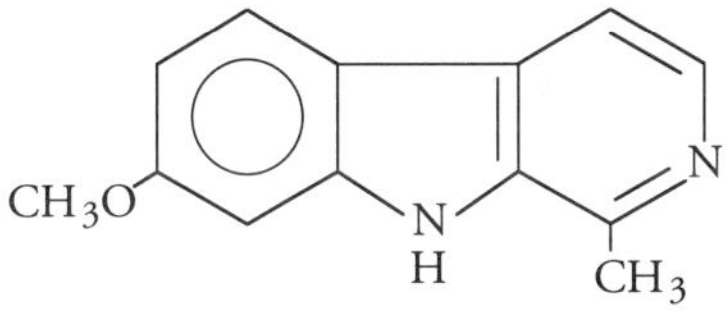

Harmine

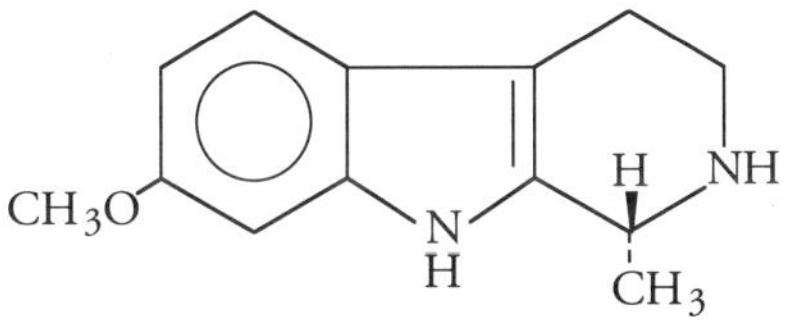

d-Leptaflorine

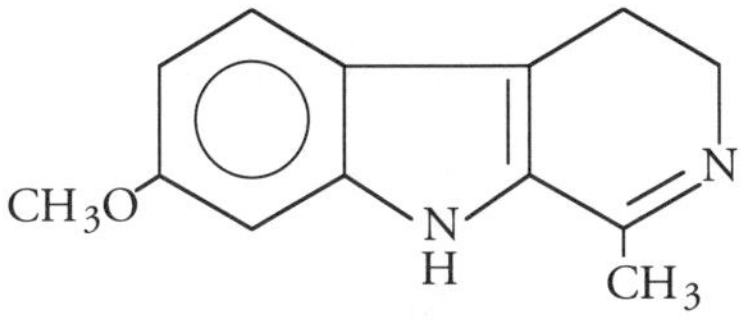

Harmaline

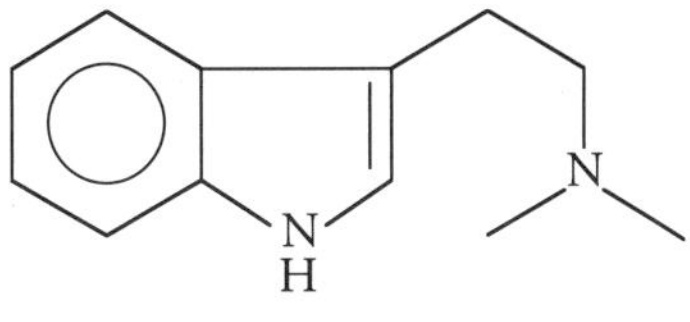

N,N-DMT

A German physician, L. Halpern, who had also employed harmine as a therapy for Parkinsonism, became the first to conduct self-experiments with the drug, in doses of up to 40 mg orally and 30 mg injected subcutaneously [Halpern 1930a,1930b]. Halpern found the injected harmine stimulating, exciting her to belligerence, she starting a fight with a man on the street, even though "the prospect for the attacker was very unfavorable"! Though she asserted her consciousness was "in no way influenced and in no way abnormal," she described it as being "packed in ether" and mentioned "lightness" and a "fleeting sensation" she "compared to the state of levitation frequently reported to occur with the crude drug *ayahuasca* or *caapi*." Not bad for something that didn't alter her consciousness! After such a promising start at the end of the twenties, interest in use of harmine as a medicament waned. Nevertheless, animal studies continued, and by the end of the thirties, A.G. Beer had studied the effects of harmine in cats, characterizing it as a central nervous system stimulant, which result would seem to be consistent with Halpern's previous self-experiments [Beer 1939a,1939b]. In a review of pharmacology of harmine-type alkaloids, J.A. Gunn also characterized harmine as a central nervous system stimulant in mammals [Gunn 1937]. Raymond-Hamet, who had reported the equivalence of telepathine and yajéine [Perrot & Raymond-Hamet 1927a,1927b], studied the "controversial" vascular effects of harmine, harmaline and leptaflorine in a dog, characterizing the drugs as vasodilators [Raymond-Hamet 1941].

A breakthrough in pharmacological studies of harmine was achieved two decades later, when the North American group of Sidney Udenfriend described harmine, 1,2,3,4-tetrahydroharmine (leptaflorine), harmaline and harman as "potent inhibitors of monoamine oxidase," (MAO-inhibitors) with an action comparable to, but more potent than the therapeutic MAO-inhibitor iproniazid [Udenfriend *et al.* 1958]. Harmine and harmaline were the most active inhibitors, with leptaflorine and harman about an order of magnitude less potent. One year later, the group of A. Pletscher suggested that the psychotropic activity of the β-carbolines from *Banisteriopsis* was due to their demonstrated activity as MAO-inhibitors [Pletscher *et al.* 1959]. We will discuss the significance of this MAO-inhibition later. In subsequent studies by Americans William M. McIsaac and Vicente Estévez, and Neil S. Buckholtz and William O. Boggan, the *ayahuasca* alkaloids were confirmed as MAO-inhibitors, along with a number of additional natural and artificial β-carbolines [Buckholtz & Boggan 1977; McIsaac & Estévez 1966].

Pharmacological studies of the β-carboline alkaloids continued. Although William J. Turner and Sidney Merlis (who later became infamous for unethical experiments with DMT and bufotenine on inmates in a mental hospital[15]) [Ott 1993], working with A. Carl, had expressed doubts that harmine was psychoactive [Turner *et al.* 1955], Harry H. Pennes and Paul H. Hoch reported that intravenous injections of 150–200 mg of harmine into hapless "mental patients" produced "visual hallucinations" in five of eleven subjects. On the other hand, these psychiatrists noted that the drug was "not hallucinogenic by the oral or subcutaneous routes," even 'though they gave as much as 960 mg orally in a single dose. Side effects (which were more pronounced by intravenous injection than by oral ingestion) included nausea, tremors and numbness, and these appeared in some subjects receiving oral harmine above a threshold of 300–400 mg [Pennes & Hoch 1957]. The Australian researchers S. Gershon and W.J. Lang later administered harmine to dogs *via* intravenous injection, claiming it provoked "apparent hallucinations" at doses of 2 mg/kg of the hydrochloride salt—it is unclear how the authors learned of the dogs' "apparent hallucinations" [Gershon & Lang 1962].

Chilean psychiatrist Claudio Naranjo then conducted the most comprehensive study of the human pharmacology of the *ayahuasca* alkaloids in the 1960s. Naranjo reported that harmine, leptaflorine (or racemic tetrahydroharmine) and harmaline were all "psychotropic," noting "I have indeed found harmaline to be hallucinogenic at dosage levels above 1 mg./kg. i.v. or 4 mg./kg. by mouth, which is about one half the threshold level for harmine... racemic tetrahydroharmine is about one-third as active as harmaline" [Naranjo 1967]. Even 'though it is of little or no importance in *ayahuasca* pharmacology, Naranjo chose to concentrate his studies with 30 volunteers on the most active compound, harmaline,[16] noting one might regard harmaline inebriation as "a syndrome shared, with minor variations, by compounds of similar structure." All of Naranjo's subjects could readily distinguish harmaline from mescaline, especially given the nausea and other uncomfortable physical symptoms only the former produced. Although previous workers had characterized harmine and related drugs as stimulants, Naranjo stated that the central effect was "hard to interpret and seems more that of a depressant." European researcher M. Maurer recently seconded this, when he characterized harmine as a mild sedative in low doses, which "caused unpleasant vegetative and neurological symptoms" at doses exceeding 300 mg [Leuner & Schlichtung 1989].

These two descriptions of harmine and harmaline as depressants are in keeping with three vague reports of effects of *Peganum harmala* seeds (which contain higher levels of harmine and harmaline than *Banisteriopsis*) described as soporific, narcotic, alcohol-like [Gunn 1937; Hassan 1967; Johnston 1855]. As noted in Chapter One, species of *Passiflora* containing these alkaloids are commonly used ethnomedicinally as sedatives and tranquilizers [Joyal 1987; Monardes 1990; Nicholson & Arzeni 1993; Oga *et al.* 1984; Speroni & Minghetti 1988]. Naranjo had stated that "the typical reaction to harmaline is a closed-eye contemplation of vivid imagery... which is in contrast to the ecstatic heavens or dreadful hells of other hallucinogens" [Naranjo 1967]. But the few first-hand reports of the effects of *ayahuasca* potions stress powerfully emotive "hallucinogenic" or entheogenic effects [Flores & Lewis 1978; Rivier & Lindgren 1972]—the ecstatic heavens and dreadful hells are most decidedly a part of the psychic territory of *ayahuasca*. As one Cashinahua Indian informant had commented: "it is a fearsome thing, I was very much afraid"

[45]

[Kensinger 1973]. Moreover, as we saw in Table II-C, of 16 *ayahuasca* potions analyzed, the average dose contained only 158 mg of β-carbolines (normally three parts harmine to one part *d*-leptaflorine, with only traces of harmaline). We will recall that in one pharmacological study 300–400 mg harmine orally was a threshold dose in human subjects and a dose of 960 mg was "not hallucinogenic" [Pennes & Hoch 1957]; whereas Naranjo found the threshold for harmine to be 8 mg/kg orally, or about 500 mg in an Indian weighing about 60 kg (with racemic leptaflorine being even less potent—we do not know if *d*-leptaflorine exceeds the racemate in potency). Even in the study of McKenna, which found the highest β-carboline levels in *ayahuasca* potions, the average level was 401 mg *per* dose (70% harmine, 24% *d*-leptaflorine, 6% harmaline), leading McKenna to comment that for an *ayahuasca* potion containing only β-carbolines to be psychoactive, "concentrations of β-carbolines considerably greater than those measured in our samples would be required" [McKenna *et al.* 1984a]. It seems obvious that the answer to this conundrum is straightforward—the main entheogenic principle of the 16 *ayahuasca* potions that have been analyzed to date is the DMT, present at levels of 25–36 mg *per* dose, with an average of 29 mg, as we saw in Table II-C. As we will discover in the next section, DMT is most decidedly an entheogen at these nominal dose levels, and definitely conducive to exploring the ecstatic heavens and the dreadful hells of the psyche.

Psychopharmacology of DMT

In April 1956, Stephen I. Szára and twenty "friends who were courageous enough to volunteer" became the first human beings to experience the entheogenic effects of the hydrochloride salt of *N,N*-dimethyltryptamine *via* intramuscular injections in doses ranging from 0.7–1.1 mg/kg body weight. Szára described the drug as having a "psychotic [*sic*] effect partially similar to that caused by meskalin or LSD-25" [Szára 1956]. DMT had been synthesized 25 years earlier, but it had not occurred to anyone to test it for entheogenic properties [Manske 1931]. It wasn't until 1955 that DMT was definitively identified as a constituent of seeds and pods of a tree in the family Leguminosae, *Anadenanthera peregrina* [Fish *et al.* 1955], the seeds of which (along with seeds of *A. colubrina*) were known to be an ingredient of a potent entheogenic snuff called *cohoba* in the Caribbean and *yopo, vilca* or *cébil* in South America [Ott 1993; Reis Altschul 1967,1972; Schultes *et al.* 1977; Wassén 1967; Wassén & Holmstedt 1963]. The finding of DMT in a natural entheogen prompted its testing, and it has since been found also to be a constituent of a widespread

Amazonian complex of entheogenic snuffs prepared from resin of numerous species of *Virola* in the family Myristicaceae, and known variously as *paricá* and *epená* [Agurell *et al.* 1969; Holmstedt 1965; Holmstedt & Lindgren 1967; Holmstedt *et al.* 1980; McKenna *et al.* 1984b; Schultes 1954b; Schultes & Hofmann 1980; Schultes & Raffauf 1990]. DMT is also known to be an entheogenic principle of a Brazilian inebriating potion called *vinho de jurema*, prepared from roots of various *Mimosa* species (also in the family Leguminosae), and it was, in fact, study of this potion which led to the first isolation in 1946 of DMT as a natural product, under the name *nigerina* or "nigerine," by Brazilian chemist O. Gonçalves de Lima, from *Mimosa hostilis* [Da Mota 1991; Gonçalves de Lima 1946; Lowie 1946; Pachter *et al.* 1959; Schultes 1979a].

Szára and his Hungarian colleagues, particularly Z. Böszörményi, G. Brunecker and A. Sai-Halász, found that within two to three minutes of injecting 50–60 mg of DMT, very impressive and potent entheogenic effects commenced, which lasted about 45 minutes to an hour [Böszörményi & Brunecker 1957; Böszörményi & Szára 1958; Szára 1957,1961], and the bizarre rapidity and potency of the drug impressed some researchers as being psychosis-like. Pursuing the idea of entheogens as *psychotomimetics*, DMT "psychopathology" was described by O.H. Arnold and G. Hofmann [1957] and the group of Sai-Halász, Brunecker and Szára characterized the drug as "ein neues Psychoticum," "a new Psychoticum," inventing a new category to go with Louis Lewin's *Euphorica, Excitantia, Hypnotica, Inebriantia*, and of course *Phantastica* [Lewin 1924; Sai-Halász *et al.* 1958]! Nevertheless, the effects Szára described hardly sounded pathological [Szára 1957]:

> Eidetic phenomena, optical illusions, pseudo-hallucinations and later real hallucinations, appeared. The hallucinations consisted of moving, brilliantly colored oriental motifs, and later I saw wonderful scenes altering very rapidly. The faces of the people seemed to be masks. My emotional state was elevated sometimes up to euphoria...

Szára did not elaborate on the differences between pseudo-hallucinations and "real" hallucinations, but perhaps anyone who has experienced entheogens first-hand will get the picture! DMT was later found to be even more potent and rapid *via* smoking the free base [Bigwood & Ott 1977]. In this case, smoking 30 mg of the drug would produce an almost instant peak entheogenic effect lasting only 5–10 minutes! In an attempt to duplicate the presumed use of DMT-containing plant extracts as enemas, Peter A.G.M. De Smet self-administered rectal doses as high as 125 mg DMT hydrochloride in 15 ml of water, with no discernible effect [De Smet 1983]. Similarly, although DMT might have been active in the *cohoba* and *epená* snuffs, intranasal administration of 5–20 mg DMT caused "no effect other than a burning sensation in the back of the nose and throat," although one patient described 10 mg intranasally as a "feeling of being 'hit on the head.'" Likewise, oral dosage of up to 350 mg "was completely without effect" [Turner & Merlis 1959], and single doses as high as a gram have been given orally, also with no effect [Shulgin 1976]. If a gram of pure DMT was without effect, then how could a mere 25–36 mg in an *ayahuasca* potion even be perceptible, much less ecstatic or fearsome?

The answer lies in the MAO-inhibiting effects of the β-carboline constituents of *ayahuasca* potions. The enzyme, monoamine oxidase, which the β-carbolines inhibit, functions in our bodies to oxidize, or decompose, compounds like the tryptamines, which otherwise might play havoc with our brain and other metabolism. Monoamine oxidase in the digestive system breaks down any DMT ingested, before it could make its way into the brain. The pharmacological mechanism of *ayahuasca* activity could be thus seen as the inhibition of monoamine oxidase by harmine and *d*-leptaflorine, thus enabling DMT to survive in our bodies long enough to be absorbed and transported to our brains. By dint of great sensitivity and insight, and an adventuresome spirit, the Amazonian shamanic psychonauts [Jünger 1970] managed to discover, with no knowledge of enzymes or alkaloids, that the nondescript *Psychotria viridis* and *Diplopterys cabrerana* leaves, normally quite innocuous, were rendered potent entheogens by boiling them in a pot with some pieces of *Banisteriopsis* stem! This, indeed, was a most ingenious piece of work, surely one of the greatest pharmacognostical discoveries of all antiquity!

Although DMT was first connected with *ayahuasca* in 1957, there were doubts about the botanical source,[17] and only when DMT was associated with plants observed in use in *ayahuasca* potions, for which botanical voucher specimens existed, in 1965 by Poisson and in 1968 by the groups of Agurell and Der Marderosian, did this mechanism for *ayahuasca* activity suggest itself to researchers [Agurell *et al.* 1968; Der Marderosian *et al.* 1968; Poisson 1965]. Poisson noted that DMT had "une action hallucinatoire fugace" ("a transient hallucinogenic activity"), when injected, but mentioned it was inactive orally. Poisson supposed that "a rather strong concentration of the active principles" or "the presence of other substances" in *natem[a]* rendered the DMT active orally [Poisson 1965]. He failed to cite the 1958 finding of Udenfriend's group, that the harmine he had isolated from *Banisteriopsis* was an MAO-inhibitor, nor did he perceive the significance of his finding of DMT in the admixture plant *Diplopterys cabrerana*, in the light of that discovery. The following year American Melvin L. Bristol published a paper on the use and preparation of an *ayahuasca* potion called *biaxíi* among the Colombian Sibundoy, one of very few Andean indigenous groups to use *ayahuasca*. Although unaware of the recent publication of Poisson's paper, Bristol cited Szára's early paper on DMT effects, noting that Hochstein and Paradies had found DMT in "leaves said to be employed in Peru along with *B. caapi* in preparing a narcotic [*sic*] beverage," leaves he took to be *Diplopterys cabrerana*. Bristol then cited the finding of the Udenfriend group, that *ayahuasca* β-carbolines were MAO-inhibitors, then reviewed the pharmacology of the β-carbolines in human beings. Having thus cited all the relevant work, he then went on to a detailed discussion of the preparation of *biaxíi* containing *B. caapi* and *chagropanga* or *Diplopterys cabrerana*, and described a ceremony in which the shaman, Salvador Chindoy, Bristol and another man each ingested some 150 ml of the potion (with half as much given to a woman present; the three men took another 75 ml 45 minutes later, but Bristol vomited and felt little or no effect). Bristol failed to make the specific connection between the MAO-inhibiting effects of *ayahuasca* alkaloids and the presumed presence of DMT in the potions, and concluded by expressing doubts whether "the *biaxíi* actually contained psychotropic methoxy-harmanes" [Bristol 1966]! Indeed, although he cited Szára's paper on DMT, he seemed to be unaware that this drug was inactive orally. The first to definitively make the connection in print between the MAO-inhibiting effects of the β-carbolines and the possible potentiation of DMT these might provoke were Swedish chemists Bo Holmstedt and Jan-Erik Lindgren. In a superb chemical investigation of South American *yopo* and *epená* snuffs and their *Anadenanthera* and *Virola* source plants, which was presented at an international symposium in San Francisco in 1967, these chemists cited Udenfriend's report of β-carbolines as MAO-inhibitors. Commenting on their finding of both tryptamines and β-carbolines in a botanically-undocumented *paricá* snuff sample from a Swedish museum, these chemists astutely concluded [Holmstedt & Lindgren 1967]:

> The occurrence of both tryptamines and β-carbolines in the South American snuffs is pharmacologically interesting. The β-carbolines are monoamine-oxidase inhibitors, and could potentiate the action of the simple indoles. The combination of β-carbolines and tryptamines would thus be advantageous.

The following year, discussing the finding of DMT in leaves of *Diplopterys cabrerana*

[49]

collected by Homer V. Pinkley, who observed their use in *ayahuasca* potions by Ecuadorian Kofán Indians, Ara Der Marderosian and his colleagues noted "many implications" of this result. They said that the practice of adding DMT-containing leaves to *ayahuasca* to "'enhance color visions' seems to be justified on a theoretical basis." Citing several reports of entheogenic properties of DMT, they rightly noted that the drug was totally inactive orally. They then concluded, as had Holmstedt and Lindgren with respect to the entheogenic snuffs, that "the harman alkaloids… are monoamine oxidase inhibitors, and perhaps this fact… may help account for the effectiveness of" the Kofán *ayahuasca* potion [Der Marderosian *et al.* 1968]. In the same issue of *American Journal of Pharmacy*, Swede Stig Agurell, collaborating with Holmstedt and Lindgren on an analysis of the same leaf material collected by Pinkley, commented plainly that "the combination in yajé of monoamine oxidase inhibiting harman alkaloids with N,N-dimethyltryptamine might result in specific pharmacological effects" [Agurell *et al.* 1968]. The subsequent finding of DMT in various *Psychotria* leaf admixtures to *ayahuasca* by Der Marderosian *et al.* [1970], Rivier and Lindgren [1972] and McKenna *et al.* [1984a] further suggested the probability of this mechanism.

The questions remained, however, *were* concentrations of β-carbolines present in *ayahuasca*, or was *ayahuasca* itself, an effective MAO-inhibitor? Furthermore, were the concentrations of DMT present in the potions orally-active at the prescribed doses? All of sixteen years were to pass before the first question was answered. Dennis J. McKenna measured the MAO-inhibition, in a "rat liver preparation," of two Peruvian *ayahuasca* samples, finding both to be "extremely effective" as MAO-inhibitors, as was also an *"ayahuasca* analogue," a mixture of 69% harmine, 26% leptaflorine and scant 5% harmaline in solution [McKenna *et al.* 1984a]. The answer accordingly was yes, *ayahuasca* potions *were* effective as MAO-inhibitors. But the human pharmacology of oral DMT remained a complete mystery. The only way convincingly to prove this proposed mechanism for *ayahuasca* pharmacology would be to conduct human bioassays with measured amounts of pure DMT and β-carbolines. As we will see, the literature on this point was virtually non-existent, thus I resolved to employ the "Heffter Technique," to don the venerable mantle of the human guinea pig… to auto-pharmacize.[18] In short, I employed the "intact Jonathan Ott preparation," my most rational bioassay in the alembic of my own brain, and plunged headlong into the phantasmagoric world of *ayahuasca*, *"ayahuasca* capsules" and *"ayahuasca* analogues." This personal "great adventure," which was to take me to the Ecuadorian Amazon and on some two dozen psychonautic expeditions into the surreal realm of the Amazonian *ambrosia*, is the subject of the third chapter.

CHAPTER THREE
Ayahuasca Analogues with Psychonautic Reports

The decade 1959–1969 had seen a burst of phytochemical activity pointing to DMT and related tryptamines (especially 5-MeO-DMT) as entheogenic principles in four major complexes of South American entheogens—in *vinho de jurema* potions prepared from *Mimosa hostilis* and other *Mimosa* species [Pachter *et al.* 1959]; in *cohoba* snuffs based on *Anadenanthera peregrina* and allied species [Agurell *et al.* 1969; Fish *et al.* 1955; Iacobucci & Rúveda 1964]; in *epená* snuffs prepared from *Virola* species [Agurell *et al.* 1969; Holmstedt 1965; Holmstedt & Lindgren 1967]; and, of course, in *ayahuasca* potions [Agurell *et al.* 1968; Der Marderosian *et al.* 1968; Der Marderosian *et al.* 1970; Poisson 1965; Rivier & Lindgren 1972]. Significantly, three of these four geographically and culturally diverse groups of South American entheogens were ingested orally (among the Witoto and nearby groups in the Colombian Amazon, the *Virola* species are used to prepare edible pellets of resin, rather than snuffs). As scientists pointed the finger at the tryptamines as active agents in these entheogens, they simultaneously evolved a theory explaining, at least in the case of *ayahuasca*, how DMT, known to be inactive orally, could be rendered a potent, oral entheogen by MAO-inhibiting β-carbolines present in *ayahuasca* potions and some snuffs [Agurell *et al.* 1968; Der Marderosian *et al.* 1968; Holmstedt & Lindgren 1967]. But nothing was known of the oral pharmacology of DMT, and for this theory to be valid, DMT would have to be at least twice as active orally as by intramuscular injection [Böszörményi & Brunecker 1957; Böszörményi & Szára 1958; Szára 1956,1957,1961], according to the analytical data on *ayahuasca* potions which began to accumulate in 1970 [Der Marderosian *et al.* 1970; Liwszyc *et al.* 1992; McKenna *et al.* 1984a; Rivier & Lindgren 1972]. The scientific world awaited an intrepid psychonaut to put the theory to the test.

American ethnobotanist Jeremy E. Bigwood became the first to step into the breach, when he conducted a single experiment a decade later, ingesting an *aya-*

huasca capsule containing 100 mg each of harmaline hydrochloride and DMT free base (equivalent to 86 mg harmaline free base or 1.0 mg/kg and 1.16 mg/kg DMT) [Bigwood 1978]. Bigwood reported the first effects within 15 minutes, increasing to a peak by 45 minutes, with "DMT like hallucinations" that "gradually tapered off," having completely disappeared 4 hours after ingestion. Of the pioneering experiment with *pharmahuasca*, Bigwood concluded:

> in short, the experience was very similar to, in both time course and effect, that of a DMT- and harmaline-containing *ayahuasca* brew that I had previously experimented with...

This, then, was an apparent confirmation of the theory of β-carboline/DMT synergy in *ayahuasca* potions, except for two problems with the experiment. First and most important is the fact that we now know harmaline to be at best a trace constituent in *ayahuasca* potions, and of little or no importance in *ayahuasca* pharmacology. As Dennis J. McKenna was to comment six years later:

> harmaline... is essentially a trace component in *ayahuasca* and probably does not contribute significantly to the MAO inhibition which this drug elicits.

McKenna, it is worth noting, had found much higher levels of harmaline, and of β-carbolines in general, than had the other groups analyzing *ayahuasca*, who had found traces or none at all [Liwszyc *et al.* 1992; McKenna *et al.* 1984a; Rivier & Lindgren 1972]. Since McKenna had found harmaline to be "slightly stronger than harmine" as an MAO-inhibitor, and since Naranjo [1967] had found plain harmaline to be fully *twice as potent* as harmine in human subjects, Bigwood's choice of harmaline for his *ayahuasca* capsule was unfelicitous and vitiated the value of his pioneering self-experiment. Which brings us to the second problem with this test, the quantities involved. While the 86 mg harmaline is well within the quantities of β-carbolines reported *per* dose in the 16 samples analyzed (which ranged from 20 to 401 mg *per* dose, with an average of 158 mg, as we saw in Table II-C), Bigwood's 100 mg DMT free base was fully *three times* the quantity found in a typical dose (a range of 25 to 36 mg, with an average of 29 mg). Thus Bigwood achieved a rough-and-ready, one-shot demonstration of the feasibility of the novel pharmacological mechanism, without realistically modeling a typical *ayahuasca* potion.

Seven years later, a series of "underground" publications made reference to

[52]

psychonautic experiments with rudimentary *ayahuasca* analogues. Although they were unaware that Schultes had contemporaneously discovered Witoto Indians in Amazonian Colombia smoking the bark and leaves of *Banisteriopsis caapi* [Schultes 1985b], "Gracie" and "Zarkov" [1985] conducted self-experiments smoking alkaloid-enriched extracts of *Peganum harmala* seeds, *Passiflora incarnata* whole plants, and *B. caapi* stems, finding:

> the high is not particularly psychedelic or hallucinogenic... One feels calm. At higher doses, dizziness and nausea sets in with very little increase in the high. Closed eye imagery is at best hypnagogic... No one who has experienced DMT or high dose mushrooms would ever call them visions...

Even 'though the group of McKenna had recently reported β-carboline quantities as high as 401 mg *per* dose of *ayahuasca*, these smoking experiments found that:

> we only needed to consume sufficient plant material for dosages in the 50 mg range... increasing the dosage did not increase the high but only aggravated the physical symptoms.

After establishing basic pharmacodynamics of smoked β-carboline-enriched plant extracts, Gracie and Zarkov experimented with smoking DMT free base ten minutes after having smoked the β-carboline preparations. They found a threefold enhancement in potency of smoked DMT with β-carboline premedication (15 mg of DMT "felt more like 35–45 mg") and a lengthened visionary period of 6 minutes instead of 2–3 minutes absent the β-carboline preparations, and heightened "almost overwhelming" auditory effects [Gracie & Zarkov 1985]. Like Bigwood's experiment, however, these data merely suggested the feasibility of tryptamine/β-carboline synergy, without modeling accurately actual *ayahuasca* potions.

These underground researchers went on to preliminary experiments involving oral ingestion of β-carboline-enriched extracts of *Peganum harmala* seeds combined with synthetic DMT free base. After various psychonautic experiments, Gracie and Zarkov concluded [1986] that:

> 5 gm of seeds with 20 mg of DMT seems to be a threshold dose... our personal preference is 7 gm of seeds with 30 mg of DMT... our nominal dose would be 10 gm of seeds with 40 mg DMT...

[53]

Here, then, were some data to sink one's teeth into... a clearcut demonstration that DMT was rendered orally-active by a β-carboline-containing plant extract at least analogous to *ayahuasca*, with oral activity demonstrated, moreover, in the 20–40 mg dose range already established in *ayahuasca* potions. On the other hand, these data did not tell us anything about β-carboline levels in the *Peganum harmala* extracts, and without analysis of the extracts employed, we have no idea if the doses were within the range found in *ayahuasca*. Indeed, *Peganum harmala* seeds have a different alkaloid profile than *Banisteriopsis caapi* stems, with harmaline often the chief alkaloid. Moreover, the seeds have been reported to contain 2–7% β-carbolines, or some 4–15 times the average concentration, 0.45%, found in 25 analyses of *B. caapi* stems. Thus Gracie and Zarkov were working with potions containing from 100 mg up to 700 mg of β-carbolines, depending on the strain and the efficiency of extraction, a rather broad range. Figuring an average of 4.5% alkaloids, their preferred dose would have contained 315 mg β-carbolines plus 30 mg DMT, exactly double the average dose of the former found in 16 samples of *ayahuasca* analyzed, with a typical average with respect to DMT. Accordingly, from these data we could deduce that the McKenna group's 401 mg β-carbolines plus 36 mg DMT in a dose of Pucallpa *ayahuasca* would likely have been active; whereas they would tell us nothing about the activity of the far lower β-carboline doses found in *ayahuasca* by the other groups [Der Marderosian *et al.* 1970; Liwszyc *et al.* 1992; Rivier & Lindgren 1972]. Clearly, more detailed, specific and repeated psychonautic experiments were required to work out the basic parameters of human pharmacodynamics of *ayahuasca* potions. Now I realized it was *my* turn to step into the breach.

TRAVELS IN THE UNIVERSE OF THE SOUL[19] WITH *AYAHUASCA*

My baseline experience with *ayahuasca* was provided by two Quijos Quichua *ayahuasqueros* from the Río Napo area of the Ecuadorian Amazon, whence had come Manuel Villavicencio's pioneering report of the entheogenic effects of *aya-huasca* in 1858. **Experiment 1** involved the ingestion in a shamanic ceremony of a potion containing *Banisteriopsis caapi* plus a small amount of leaves of *Ilex guayusa*—no tryptamine-rich leaf admixture was employed. I had not witnessed the preparation of the potion, but the *ayahuasquero* told me in Spanish that it contained about a handful of *guayusa* leaves to yield a total of some 20 doses. Ingestion of some 60 ml of this potion produced a dreamy sedation with no visionary or entheogenic effects. The shaman explained the addition of *guayusa* leaves as designed to counteract the soporific effects of the *ayahuasca*, although for me their caffeine content was insufficient for that purpose, and I had to fight off sleep. I could see why β-carboline-enriched plant infusions had been used traditionally in Ecuador, Brazil, México, France, Italy, the United States and elsewhere as sedatives, effects which have been corroborated in modern pharmacological investigations [Joyal 1987; Monardes 1990; Moore 1989; Oga *et al.* 1984; Speroni & Minghetti 1988; Weiss 1988].

Experiment 2 consisted of a similar potion prepared by the same *ayahuasquero*, to which had been added, *per* request, leaves of *amirucapanga, Psychotria viridis.* This gave virtually the same result, although there was a vague hint, perhaps psychological, of the presence of stimulating DMT. When I questioned the shaman regarding the preparation of the potion (he had not wished to prepare it in the presence of strangers), he told me he had added a handful of leaves for the entire batch, again yielding some 20 doses. This could not have represented more than a few leaves *per* dose, and it is not surprising that again, the effect was hypnotic and not entheogenic. Evidently this shaman was not accustomed to the use of DMT-rich leaves in his *ayahuasca.*

For **Experiment 3**, a different Quijos Quichua *ayahuasquero* was invited, and he agreed to prepare the potion in front of us. This preparation was as described on page 17, but the cooking time was intermediate, some 5 hours, similar to what had been reported by Bristol among the Colombian Sibundoy [Bristol 1966]. Unlike the Sibundoy, however, who extract only the bark shavings of the *Banisteriopsis* stems, this Quijos Quichua *ayahuasquero* had *discarded* the bark shavings, and extracted the yellowish stems themselves, which were quartered. There was no way precisely to weigh the amount of liana, but a pot with roughly a 20 liter capacity was filled up with stem pieces covered with water, with again, only a handful of *amirucapanga* leaves for the whole pot, all 20 doses. Anticipating this possibility, I had already prepared an infusion equivalent to about 50 *Psychotria viridis* leaves *per* dose, thrice extracted with water and boiled down to roughly 700 ml. I diffidently explained to the *ayahuasquero*, who was hovering over his *ayahuasca* pot, that we were particularly interested in experiencing the effects of *amirucapanga*, and to that end I had concentrated the essence of the leaves into a tea, which I held up gingerly for his inspection. Without hesitation, he said "what a good idea!" and immediately added most of the liquid to his *ayahuasca* pot! Although surprised that he would so readily assent to adding an infusion of unknown strength to his potion, and what is more, one prepared by a rank *amateur,* I was delighted at his open-mindedness, and rejoiced in the knowledge that this time we would experience the stimulation and visionary qualities latent in the unassuming *amirucapanga* leaves. The rest of the preparation of the potion was uneventful, and that night we were each given doses "eyeballed" by the shaman—I received about 50 ml.

The potion was far from delectable but went down easily for those who had cut their entheogenic teeth on *péyotl* and *teonanácatl*, and we were all given a piece of ginger rhizome (*Zingiber officinale*) to kill the taste. Despite its Asiatic origin, ginger has been adopted in northwest Amazonia as a medicinal plant, and Ecuadorian Quichuas reportedly use ginger juice on cataplasms for infected eyes [Schultes & Raffauf 1990]. This time there was no question that the potion was powerfully entheogenic. Within an hour I experienced vivid visions and synæsthesia, with a pronounced auditory component. Even 'though the powerful and characteristic effects of DMT moved forcefully into the foreground (I had already had many experiences with smoked DMT free base), there was a noticeable sedation from the harmine and other *ayahuasca* alkaloids—I recall thinking, with astonishment, that sleep would perhaps have been possible in the midst of the DMT *maelström*; and indeed, the shaman cautioned us not to lie down, lest we slumber. Very euphoric and quite powerful DMT effects lasted for some two hours; the first a consistent plateau level; the second a gentle descent from the treetop realm of *Sacha Runa* to Gæa's ground zero, after which I slept easily and soundly.

Based purely on subjective effects, and lacking any analytical data on the three potions, I was left with the distinct impression that plain *ayahuasca* was a sedative/hypnotic, potentially useful as a tranquilizer, like harmine-, harmaline- and leptaflorine-containing *Passiflora* species which have found such use world-wide. I was also convinced that *ayahuasca* potions were indeed capable of rendering DMT active orally, and that DMT represented the stimulating, entheogenic constituent of the *ayahuasca* potions which had been submitted to quantitative chemical analysis. Based on my initial experiences in Amazonia, I decided not only that the DMT-rich leaf admixtures strengthened the visionary potency of the potions, but that, as the Sharanahua and Culina Indians of Perú told Rivier and Lindgren, one would probably see nothing interesting without this crucial ingredient, or one or another of the known entheogenic solanaceous, acanthaceous or amaranthaceous plant admixtures to *ayahuasca*. I was not alone in this assessment—D.J. McKenna had concluded that "DMT… is probably reponsible for the hallucinogenic effects of *ayahuasca*" and Luna and Amaringo (himself an experienced *ayahuasquero*) put it thus: "the alkaloid responsible for the psychoactivity of the brew was most probably dimethyltryptamine, the alkaloids in *Banisteriopsis caapi* not being a large enough dose to elicit hallucinations" [Luna & Amaringo 1991; McKenna *et al.* 1986]. The fact that a "traditional pharmacopœia" of some 97 plants had been reported as *ayahuasca* admixtures (see Table I) [McKenna *et al.* 1986], of which at least a dozen were known entheogenic plants falling into some four different pharmacological categories, suggested to me an analogy to the pre-Columbian Mexican *cacáhuatl* potions based on aqueous extracts of *cacaoaquáuitl* or *Theobroma cacao*, to which were added entheogenic mushrooms and other sacred drugs, apart from more prosaic medicaments [Ott 1985]. I resolved to attempt to elucidate in detail the human pharmacology of the DMT-containing *ayahuasca* potions.

Since I planned also experiments with *ayahuasca* analogues based on substituting readily-available (and far more potent) *harmel* (*Peganum harmala*) seeds for stems of *ayahuasca*, I next turned my attention to that drug. For **Experiment 4**, I ingested a potion prepared by extracting with 30% lime juice in water (the acidic lime juice to enhance alkaloid solubility in water) 15 grams of ground *harmel* seeds. The seeds were hand ground in a porcelain mortar, then placed in a small pot with sufficient lime juice/water to suspend them, then brought rapidly to a boil with stirring. I then filtered the suspension with a *Melitta*-type single-cup coffee filter holder containing a reusable gold-metal-mesh filter element (paper will also work fine). The marc (the residual solid matter) was then added back to the pot and again extracted by the same means, with a minimal quantity of lime juice/water, stirred and brought quickly to a boil. I don't recommend prolonged heating or use of large amounts of water followed by prolonged heating to concentrate. After filtration of the second extract, a small quantity of water was used to rinse the pot and poured over the marc. I ended up with about 150 ml of extract looking rather like unfiltered apple juice, with a somewhat unpleasant, but hardly disgusting taste. The whole extraction procedure took only about 15–20 minutes.

Within an hour of ingesting the *harmel* extract it was obvious the seeds were psychoactive, and they elicited a mild sedative effect which attained a peak in potency 2 hours after ingestion and had mostly dissipated at the 4 hour point. There were no visionary or entheogenic effects, only a bit of visual "tailing" when something moved before my eyes. Tinnitus and a mild numbing sensation accompanied a slowed heartbeat and mild vertigo when I closed my eyes. Despite this sedation, I slept fitfully, and awoke the next day with a hangover which lasted all day. There was no nausea or overt negative effects, but the experience was hard on my body, and I had no desire to repeat it. It was similar to **Experiment 1** in Ecuador with DMT-less *ayahuasca*, and I estimated the dose could have represented between 300 and 1050 mg of β-carbolines, probably closer to the upper limit, based on comparisons with Naranjo's findings [1967].

Having isolated and purified DMT as the free base from *Desmanthus illinoensis* (the thin-layer chromatographic properties and melting point commensurate with synthetic material), I subsequently turned my attention to experiments with known amounts of DMT. For **Experiment 5**, I prepared an extract of 5 g *harmel* seeds (using the procedure outlined above), and added 20 mg of DMT free base (0.25 mg/kg) to the 100 ml of hot, acidic extract, and immediately quaffed this. The estimated quantity of β-carbolines would be 100–350 mg, or 1.25–4.38 mg/kg. This provoked a definite stimulation from the DMT, a feeling of aliveness and excitement in decided contrast to the deadbeat feeling plain *harmel* seed extract had provoked in me. However, I couldn't say it was really a distinct DMT effect, and marked it down as subthreshold with regard to entheogenic effects. It reminded me somewhat of **Experiment 2** in Ecuador, with more stimulation from the DMT.

I was eager to proceed to **Experiment 6**, in which I extracted only 4 g of *harmel* seeds, whose effects I wished to minimize, and this time added 30 mg of DMT free base, representing 0.38 mg/kg (with an estimated β-carboline level of 80–280 mg, probably closer to the upper limit; 1.0–3.5 mg/kg). This time there were distinct, but threshold-level, entheogenic effects of DMT commencing 1:10 after ingestion, building rapidly to a peak at 1:15; holding a plateau until 2:00; descending to baseline level by 3:00. There were vivid colored patterns with eyes opened or closed, euphoric exhilaration and general stimulation alloyed with *harmel* seed sedation, which led me to yawn repeatedly. This was more like **Experiment 3** in Ecuador, but significantly less potent, and I estimated also that the oral potency of DMT was about half or less than its potency when smoked (itself twice the potency when injected i.m.), 'though it was difficult to compare based on the radically-different pharmacodynamics of the different routes of ingestion. I could thus say that the threshold level for oral DMT in *ayahuasca* was between 0.25 and 0.38 mg/kg, and that 1.0–3.5 mg/kg β-carbolines was the probable MAO-inhibitor threshold.

In order more precisely to determine the β-carboline threshold, I extracted harmine, for further experiments, from *Peganum harmala* seeds, and purified it as the hydrochloride salt, yielding greenish crystals melting at 262°C. I decided to hold the DMT level at the known entheogenic threshold of 30 mg, and to start my series of *pharmahuasca* capsules with 30 mg DMT plus 40 mg harmine (as free base; equal to 47 mg harmine HCl), that being the level Rivier and Lindgren had established as an average for Río Purús *ayahuasca*. For **Experiment 7**, I ingested a gelatine capsule containing these quantities, and felt little; only a slight sensation of activity. Reasoning that the Culina and Sharanahua Indians from the Río Purús area must have weighed on average 60 kg, and that their 40 mg β-carboline average accordingly corresponded to 0.67 mg/kg, I prepared another capsule with 30 mg

DMT free base plus 63 mg harmine HCl, or 54 mg harmine base; 0.67 mg/kg for me. In **Experiment 8**, I ingested this capsule, again feeling little, although I could sense the presence of the DMT. I next increased the harmine HCl to 70 mg (=60 mg base, 0.75 mg/kg) and ingested this in a capsule for **Experiment 9** with 30 mg DMT free base. Now there was a more detectable DMT stimulation, but still well below the entheogenic threshold I had experienced with the same amount of DMT combined with infusions of 4 g *harmel* seeds.

I again increased the harmine HCl to 94 mg (=80 mg base; 1.0 mg/kg) and in **Experiment 10** ingested this quantity in a *pharmahuasca* capsule with 30 mg DMT. The results were similar to the previous experiment; a definite stimulation from DMT, slightly more intense this time, but still not attaining what I could characterize as an entheogenic threshold-level experience. Similarly, **Experiment 11**, with 30 mg DMT plus 117 mg harmine HCl (=100 mg harmine base; 1.25 mg/kg), while slightly more intense with regard to DMT stimulation, still was clearly short of the threshold attained with 30 mg DMT plus 4 g *harmel* seed infusion.

Finally, in **Experiment 12**, combining 35 mg DMT free base with 141 mg of harmine HCl (=120 mg base; 1.5 mg/kg), I made the entheogenic grade. When weighing out the DMT, a chunk had fallen on the balance bringing the weight up to 35 mg instead of the customary 30 (0.44 mg/kg) and I had decided to "go with the flow" and use this quantity. Within 45 minutes of ingesting my sixth *pharmahuasca* capsule, it was clear to me that the threshold would be attained, and I experienced a distinct, but mild, entheogenic DMT effect building to a peak by 1:05 after ingestion and maintaining a plateau until 1:50; with the effects characteristically tapering off gradually and virtually disappearing by 3 hours after ingestion. The experience was of comparable intensity to **Experiment 6**, 30 mg DMT plus infusions of 4 g *harmel* seeds, and both were decidedly less potent than my **Experiment 3** in Ecuador, which evidently involved a higher DMT dose. I therefore concluded that the threshold to effect sufficient MAO-inhibition, as to render DMT active orally, was 1.5 mg/kg harmine. For me, as an 80 kg individual, the threshold for an *ayahuasca*-type effect was 120 mg harmine free base plus 30 mg DMT free base (1.5 mg/kg of the former; 0.38 mg/kg of the latter).

To reconfirm this finding, in **Experiment 13** I increased the amounts of both compounds, to 188 mg harmine HCl (=160 mg base; 2.0 mg/kg) with 40 mg DMT free base (0.5 mg/kg). Indeed, this evoked a proportionally stronger DMT effect with first signs evident only 20 minutes after ingesting and the peak attained at 1:30, maintaining a plateau until 2:40, with clearly diminishing effects at the 3 hour point, and no effects at all by the fourth hour. This experience was still, however, less potent than my **Experiment 3** in Ecuador. To make certain that what I was experiencing was the effect of DMT rendered active orally, I conducted a control **Experiment 14** with 141 mg harmine HCl (=120 mg of base; 1.5 mg/kg) with no DMT. This provoked no entheogenic effects or stimulation, just a slightly perceptible *harmel*-type sedation which was still evident several hours later, but sufficiently mild as to make me forget I had ingested anything. This, then, was convincing proof that a barely-perceptible sedative dose of harmine was indeed capable of effecting sufficient MAO-inhibition to render DMT, in the quantities present in *ayahuasca* potions, entheogenic by the oral route of administration.

This established, I next turned my attention to *ayahuasca* analogues. For clarity I will present my results in a logical, but not necessarily chronological sequence; that is, I will not describe the rest of my experiments in order. Going back to *harmel* seeds, one of the most potent and most readily-available sources of the β-carbolines, I next took advantage of the collaboration of several fellow psychonauts to conduct a comparative experiment. In **Experiment 18**, five individuals ingested *ayahuasca* analogues with a standard amount of dried *Psychotria viridis* leaves, but with variable amounts of *Peganum harmala* seeds. Each potion contained an extract of 20 g *P. viridis* leaves, but combined with 1,2,3 and 4 g *harmel* seeds (two individuals had 4 g *harmel* seeds). The ground seeds were combined with the powdered leaves (reduced to coarse powder in a blender), and extracted twice with 30% lemon juice, bringing quickly to a boil under stirring, as already described. The 20 g of leaves would be expected to yield 40 mg DMT according to the average presented in Table II-B. Owing to lack of glassware and primitive conditions for the workup, there was apparently an inefficient extraction of the DMT from the leaves, since only one psychonaut reported visions, whereas the rest had definite DMT stimulation which was, however, not quite threshold-level for entheogenic effects. Significantly, however, we all experienced roughly a similar level of activity, and the only person to report visions had the potion prepared with 2 g *harmel* seed (I had ingested the potion with 1 g seed). This suggests that there is a very definite β-carboline threshold, and that there may be no advantage in increasing amounts of this component; that it is rather the DMT which is determinant, once the threshold for MAO-inhibition has been crossed. I accordingly settled on 3 g of *harmel* seed as a standard amount for *ayahuasca* analogues, to allow sufficient leeway given the known variability of alkaloid levels in *harmel* seeds, since the strain I've been using appears to be on the upper end of the potency scale. I also decided in the future to extract the plant matter three times, to ensure quantitative extraction of alkaloids.

For **Experiment 19**, I prepared a potion by three times extracting 3 g *harmel* seeds in 30% lime juice, yielding a total of 100 ml of extract (estimated content of 60–210 mg β-carbolines; average of 135 mg or 1.7 mg/kg), to which I added 40 mg DMT free base (0.5 mg/kg). Entheogenic effects of DMT commenced about 1:10 after ingestion and built to a peak by 1:15, maintaining a plateau until 2:15, with the slow descent to 3:00, when effects had more or less disappeared. On a five-point potency scale, with 1 representing non-entheogenic stimulation; 2 representing the entheogenic threshold; 3 corresponding to a mild trip; 4 representing a moderately-strong trip; with 5 representing a technical knockout of the ego; I rated this experiment a solid "3." This compares to the "1" in **Experiment 5** (20 mg DMT; 0.25 mg/kg), and the "2" in **Experiment 6** (30 mg DMT; 0.38 mg/kg). Although **Experiment 5** had involved extracts of 5 g *harmel* and **Experiment 6** employed 4 g, this variable would appear to be insignificant.

Experiment 20 consisted of the 3 extracts of 3 g *harmel* seed combined with 50 mg DMT (0.63 mg/kg) and **Experiment 21** involved the typical *harmel* seed extract to which 60 mg DMT (0.75 mg/kg) was added. Whereas 60 mg DMT represented a "4" the 50 mg DMT dose was in between a "3" and a "4." I was thus able to establish a more or less linear increase in entheogenic potency as the DMT levels were increased; from the merely stimulating (0.25 mg/kg) to the entheogenic threshold (0.38 mg/kg); with 0.5 mg/kg constituting a mild trip, up to a moderately-strong trip at 0.75 mg/kg DMT. These data are summarized in Table III-A.

TABLE III–A
HUMAN PHARMACOLOGY OF *AYAHUASCA* ANALOGUE (*P. HARMALA*/DMT)

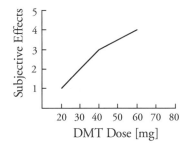

Variable Amounts of DMT With 3-Times Extraction of Ground *Peganum harmala* L. Seeds: [5g, 4g, 3g, 3g, 3g]

The results of my seven *pharmahuasca* capsule experiments, with variable amounts of harmine from 40 mg to 160 mg (0.5 to 2.0 mg/kg) are presented in Table III-B. With the exception of the last two experiments (Experiments 12 and 13), the amount of DMT was held constant at 30 mg (0.38 mg/kg).

In my first foray into all-analogue *ayahuasca* (compounded exclusively of non-traditional ingredients), I experimented with *Peganum harmala* seeds combined with *Desmanthus illinoensis* root bark. Roots of the "Illinois bundleflower" were recently reported to contain 0.18% DMT plus 0.06% of inactive *N*-monomethyltryptamine (MMT) [Thompson *et al.* 1987]. Almost all of the tryptamines were concentrated in the root bark, which made up about half the weight of the dried roots. For **Experiment 15**, I combined 4 g of ground *Peganum harmala* seeds with 27.6 g of ground *Desmanthus illinoensis* root, calculated to contain about 50 mg DMT. The material was extracted thrice with about 100 ml boiling 30% lime juice, filtering each time. The resulting 250 ml potion was drunk, giving me a subthreshold, mildly stimulating effect of DMT. Accordingly, for **Experiment 16**, I doubled the

TABLE III–B
HUMAN PHARMACOLOGY OF *AYAHUASCA* CAPSULES (HARMINE-VARIABLE)

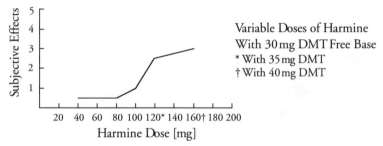

quantity of *D. illinoensis* root to 57.6 g, the bark of which was ground and combined with 4 g of ground *P. harmala* seed, and thrice extracted as before. This time the *ayahuasca* analogue gave a distinct entheogenic effect of DMT commencing at 0:30 and building to a peak at 1:15 with a 30 minute plateau. Two hours after ingestion the effects had noticeably diminished, and an hour later had all but disappeared. This was threshold-level for entheogenic DMT effects, comparable to **Experiment 12**. Evidently the strain of *D. illinoensis* which I had in hand (which had been purchased on the commercial herb market) was somewhat lower in tryptamines than the strain analyzed in 1987. In order to demonstrate the feasibility of attaining more solid entheogenic effects from this *ayahuasca* analogue, I conducted **Experiment 22** with an extract (by standard procedure) of 3 g ground *P. harmala* seeds plus 50 g ground root bark of *D. illinoensis* (a different strain; equivalent to roughly 85 g whole dried root; dried, ground root bark is now commercially available). This potion provoked a slightly stronger, distinct but threshold-level entheogenic effect with typical pharmacokinetics. For **Experiment 24**, I increased the quantity of *D.*

illinoensis root bark powder to 60 g, equivalent to approximately 100 g dried root. This potion effected a more potent DMT trip, again with typical latency period and characteristic duration of plateau and of the overall experience.

I decided to make another *ayahuasca* analogue utilizing again *Peganum harmala* as source of β-carbolines, this time combined with leaves of *Acacia phlebophylla* as the tryptamine source. The leaves of this Australian *Acacia* were reported 25 years ago to contain about 0.3% DMT, nearly double the concentration found in *Desmanthus illinoensis* roots, and intermediate in concentration between the traditional Amazonian leaf additives *Diplopterys cabrerana* and *Psychotria* spp. (see Table II-B) [Rovelli & Vaughan 1967]. From the *Alt. Drugs* bulletin board system on the *Internet* computer network, there had already been a posting describing an entheogenic *ayahuasca* analogue utilizing "a heaped teaspoon of ground harmala seeds" swallowed neat and chased 10 minutes later by an infusion of an unspecified quantity of *Acacia phlebophylla* leaves [Greenwood 1993]. The intrepid Australian psychonaut characterized this as "nothing short of the most amazing and intense experience of my life to date." For **Experiment 23** I prepared a potion by thrice extracting 3 g ground *P. harmala* seeds together with 20 g ground *A. phlebophylla* leaves. The resulting 150 ml potion provoked a rapid DMT effect of moderate strength commencing at 0:30 and peaking by 1:00, with a half-hour plateau and two hour descent to baseline by 3:30. In potency this was comparable to my **Experiment 21** with 60 mg pure DMT, which is the DMT quantity 20 g of *Acacia phlebophylla* would be expected to contain.

PARALLEL EXPERIMENTS AND CORROBORATIVE DATA

Parallel psychonautic experiments by several colleagues have confirmed and extended my *pharmahuasca* studies, using both harmaline and 6-methoxy-harmalan *in lieu* of harmine as the enzyme inhibitor, and furthermore employing 5-MeO-DMT and the artificial *N,N*-diethyltryptamine (DET) [Ott 1993] *in lieu* of DMT as the entheogenic ingredient. These experiments, which will be outlined below, showed a pattern of activity consistent with what I had already established.

American biochemist J.C. Callaway had independently conducted a series of psychonautic experiments parallel to my own. Callaway has been working on mammalian metabolism of endogenous tryptamines and β-carbolines, and has elaborated a hypothesis to explain dreams *via* nocturnal interactions of tryptamines and β-carbolines, what we might call "endogenous *ayahuasca*" or *endohuasca* [Callaway 1988, 1993]. Callaway kindly provided me the notes of his *pharmahuasca* studies, including one experiment he conducted *on the same day* as my **Experiment 12** (my first *pharmahuasca* experiment to give me unequivocal *ayahuasca*-like effects). Callaway ingested a *pharmahuasca* capsule containing 10 mg 5-MeO-DMT combined with 70 mg harmaline expressed as free base (equivalent to 1.2 mg/kg harmaline, similar to the level Bigwood found active). Since 5-MeO-DMT is roughly four times the potency of DMT when smoked [Ott 1993], Callaway's dose of that compound would be equivalent to 40 mg DMT, or 0.69 mg/kg. Callaway felt the first effects in 18 minutes and distinct psychoactive effects by 45 minutes, which built to a peak by 1:25, with a plateau until the 1:58 point, when the effects were diminishing [Callaway 1992]. We may conclude from this experiment that harmaline is somewhat more active than harmine as MAO-inhibitor, which biochemical data bears out [McKenna *et al.* 1984a]. Furthermore, we may deduce that 5-MeO-DMT can substitute for DMT as the entheogenic agent in *ayahuasca*. Much as smoked 5-MeO-DMT is some four times the potency of smoked DMT, it appears also to show about four times the oral activity in combination with β-carbolines. Callaway reported no color visions, again mirroring the activity of 5-MeO-DMT when smoked—this compound is often likened to DMT "without the movie." A European researcher, M. Markus, also found 5-MeO-DMT to provoke "hallucinatory effects" in oral combination with harmine, harmaline or 6-methoxy-harmalan in *pharmahuasca* capsules [Leuner & Schlichtung 1989].

Another colleague has independently conducted psychonautic experiments with harmaline as enzyme inhibitor, using both DMT and DET as entheogenic agents. It must be noted that the harmaline hydrochloride used by this researcher was later determined by analysis to be a mixture of some two parts harmaline to one part harmine (see Note 14). After establishing that 175 mg harmaline hydrochloride (equivalent to 146 mg base, or 2.25 mg/kg) was only a mild sedative, this psychonaut went on to combining 150 mg harmaline (130 mg base, 2.0 mg/kg) with a like quantity of DET free base (2.3 mg/kg), a short-acting tryptamine roughly equipotent with DMT *via* smoking or injection. In all experiments in this series, the tryptamine was taken 10–20 minutes after taking the β-carboline. This quantity was "definitely an overdosage," with major entheogenic effects commencing at the 1:30 point and lasting for several hours (DET normally lasts much longer than DMT; some two hours rather than 10 minutes... a European colleague had similarly reported a "very strong effect" from a *pharmahuasca* capsule prepared with 150 mg harmine HCl in combination with 60 mg DET). Going on to experiments with DMT, this brave psychonaut found 50 mg harmaline hydrochloride (43 mg base; 0.66 mg/kg) combined with 60 mg DMT (0.92 mg/kg) to be inactive. Quantities were increased to 100 mg harmaline HCl (86 mg base; 1.32 mg/kg) and 120 mg DMT (1.85 mg/kg), provoking an entheogenic effect starting at 1:20, peaking rapidly and starting to recede at 2:30, being mostly over by 4:00. This psychonaut then went on to decrease the quantities of DMT to 80 mg (1.23 mg/kg) and 35 mg (0.54 mg/kg) in subsequent tests, in combination with 150 mg harmaline salt (130 mg base; 2.0 mg/kg). Both dose levels again produced entheogenic effects. In five tests, accordingly, this psychonaut established that 1.32–2.0 mg/kg of the harmaline/harmine mixture was sufficient to activate tryptamines, whereas 0.66 mg/kg was not, even in combination with 60 mg DMT, far more than has ever been found in a dose of *ayahuasca* and at 0.92 mg/kg, nearly triple the tryptamine threshold I had already established. These tests thus confirm my finding that there is a definite threshold of β-carbolines for an *ayahuasca* effect. As in Callaway's case, these tests show the harmaline threshold may be a bit lower than that for harmine, 1.2–1.32 mg/kg in these studies, but close to the 1.5 mg/kg I had established for harmine.

Another interesting finding by this psychonaut was that 250 mg harman hydrochloride (equivalent to 209 mg base or 3.2 mg/kg) was ineffective as MAO-inhibitor in *pharmahuasca* when combined with 35 mg DMT (0.54 mg/kg; an active level). This is surprising, since harman was about as active as harmaline and harmine in *in vitro* tests of MAO-inhibition, and is useful as a *caveat*—it is not always possible to extrapolate test results from the laboratory to the real world, or from one species to another (see Table IV-A, Note 1). Yohimbine hydrochloride was also shown to be ineffective as a *pharmahuasca* MAO-inhibitor at 54 and 80 mg doses in combination with 60 and 120 mg DMT.

Of compelling interest also in this psychonautic series were two preliminary experiments with 150 mg harmaline salt (130 mg base; 2.0 mg/kg) in combination with 60 and 100 mg mescaline hydrochloride (51 and 86 mg base or 0.78 and 1.32 mg/kg respectively). In the first case there were definite subthreshold effects of mescaline, and in the second case a pronounced threshold effect of mescaline was felt! While mescaline is itself entheogenic, it is active at 3.0–5.0 mg/kg, and this experiment suggests that *peyohuasca* is possible—a definite potentiation of the too-weak mescaline with β-carbolines. I had already suspected this, inasmuch as Sharanahua Indians of Perú add pieces of an *Opuntia* cactus to their *ayahuasca*, to make "the effects very strong" (see pages 22–23), and several *Opuntia* species are known to contain low levels of mescaline, pharmacologically insignificant in absence of some potentiation [Ott 1993]. This hunch is thereby borne out experimentally. Curiously, the myth has been promulgated in the drug "scene" that β-phenethylamines like mescaline are a potentially deadly combination with β-carbolines, which is clearly

[65]

not so, as the above-cited experiments underscore (this psychonaut had also combined β-carbolines with the artificial β-phenethylamine 2,4,5-trimethoxy-β–phenethylamine, but there were few effects). Callaway, for example, warned that such a combination "may result in life threatening situations" [Callaway 1993]. There is absolutely no evidence for this, as I confirmed by questioning phenethylamine expert Alexander T. Shulgin [1993]. This myth apparently results from a confusion between dietary restrictions correctly associated with long-term medicinal use of *irreversible* MAO-inhibitors, and the entirely unrelated, purely spiritual, rather than pharmacological, dietary restrictions *sometimes* associated with the use of *ayahuasca* in Amazonia. We will return to this point after examining the use of medicinal MAO-inhibitors, and their potential as activators in *pharmahuasca*.

MEDICINAL MAO-INHIBITORS AND *PHARMAHUASCA*

MAO-inhibitors are widely used in medicine as anti-depressants, typically in long-term therapy involving daily administration of irreversible inhibitors. In order to ascertain whether medicinal MAO-inhibitors might be useful components of *pharmahuasca*, I resolved to combine DMT with the pharmaceutical MAO-inhibitor isocarboxazid (5-methyl-3-isoxazole carboxylic acid-2-benzylhydrazide) or *Marplan*. This medicament is ordinarily given in a dose of 30 mg daily (once, or 10 mg three times), and the resulting chronic increase in serotonine in the brain follows a latency period of a few days to a few months and persists for a like time after ceasing administration of the drug. Euphoric reactions to this treatment are rare, and are considered to be adverse side-effects! For **Experiment 17**, I took 30 mg *Marplan* in three 10 mg doses at 9:00, 14:00 and 19:00, and an hour after the last dose took 30 mg DMT free base in a capsule. A mild but distinct DMT effect commenced 35 minutes after ingestion of the capsule, built to a peak by 1:10, with a plateau to 1:40, declining over the next hour. Thus it is indeed possible to make *pharmahuasca* with medicinal MAO-inhibitors, at least with *Marplan*. This compound, which is an irreversible MAO-inhibitor (in contrast to the β-carbolines, which are reversible), appears moreover to be several times the potency of the natural *ayahuasca* alkaloids.

This finding contrasted with an experiment conducted three decades ago, in which DMT was adminstered after chronic MAO-inhibition had been effected with the medicinal MAO-inhibitor iproniazid or *Marsilid* (1-isonicotinyl-2-isopropylhydrazine). This compound was originally used in medicine as an anti-tuberculosis agent, and in 1952 it was observed to be a stimulant in some patients, an effect later associated with its efficacy as an MAO-inhibitor. In this case, subjects were pretreated with 100 mg iproniazid daily for four days. After two drug-free days (to eliminate direct effects of iproniazid, whereas the MAO-inhibition would still persist), the subjects were given 0.35–0.83 mg/kg DMT *via* intramuscular injection [Sai-Halász 1963]. Paradoxically, the subjects experienced *decreased* effects of DMT, compared to a previous experiment in which they had been given the drug absent MAO-inhibition, and "had an odd feeling of a changed personality" which the researchers likened to the symptoms presaging a psychotic break. Of course, this was not a *pharmahuasca* experiment, and rather involved the effect of MAO-inhibition on *injected* DMT. This experiment had been conducted to follow up on the finding that pretreatment with the potent serotonine antagonist methysergide or UML-491 (1-methyl-*d*-lysergic acid butanolamide; see Ott 1993 for details on this LSD analogue), known commercially as *Sansert*, had "a strong potentiating effect" on DMT [Sai-Halász 1962]. The same subjects had been given 1–2 mg "antiserotonin" (*Sansert*) orally (or 0.5 mg intramuscularly; either dose being below the entheogenic threshold for this drug) 30–40 minutes before being injected with 0.81–0.89 mg/kg DMT (the same dose they had already received neat—some of the subjects were given 50–80% of this DMT dose on the second occasion, after pretreatment with *Sansert*). Even the reduced dose with *Sansert* pretreatment was experienced as more potent by some subjects, while most of those who had the same dose with and without *Sansert* had "very intense aggravation of the symptoms." Of course, *Sansert* is itself entheogenic, but the threshold for such effect is well above that employed in this experiment. It seems that serotonine *inhibition* potentiates the effect of injected DMT, whereas MAO-inhibition would be rather expected to *increase* serotonine concentration in the brain. In all events, these experiments have little applicability to *ayahuasca*, where the key MAO-inhibition takes place in the digestive system, not in the brain, enabling the DMT to be absorbed into the bloodstream, thence finding its way to the brain. On the other hand, the finding that an MAO-inhibitor *decreased* the activity of injected DMT (and that it was serotonine *inhibition*, not the *increased* brain serotonine fostered by use of MAO-inhibitors, which enhanced the effect of DMT), may be important in *ayahuasca* pharmacology. It is at least possible that, while *ayahuasca* MAO-inhibitors enable DMT to survive the rigors of the gut and be thus rendered active orally, they may exert an *anti-DMT effect* in the brain, which might help explain why oral DMT is much less active than DMT smoked. On the other hand, Gracie and Zarkov [1985] had reported that smoked DMT was potentiated by prior smoking of β-carboline-enriched plant extracts, but this experiment involved smoking, not ingesting the alkaloids, as would be the case in *ayahuasca*, and is not applicable here. Not only is the sedative effect of the β-carbolines undesirable, but we have at least cause to suspect these compounds of having a paradoxical effect antagonistic to DMT in the brain. The lesson here is that the β-carboline component of *ayahuasca* should be minimized; that ironically, we need less *ayahuasca* in our *ayahuasca*!

It should also be pointed out that some tryptamines are themselves MAO-inhibitors. Both α-methyltryptamine (or IT-290) and α-ethyltryptamine (or etryptamine) were found to have the same potency as iproniazid as MAO-inhibitors [Grieg *et al.* 1959], and the latter was used in the 1950s along with iproniazid as a medicinal MAO-inhibitor before more specific and less toxic agents were discovered. IT-290 is a long-lasting stimulant in 20 mg doses, whereas etryptamine has a shorter duration following 150 mg doses [Ott 1993; Shulgin & Shulgin 1994]. It is likely there'd be oral synergy between either of these compounds and DMT. DMT and 5-MeO-DMT show weak MAO-inhibiting effects [McKenna *et al.* 1984b].

In a startling recent development, a point mutation (resulting in the deletion of a glutamine residue at the end of the amino acid chain of the enzyme coded by one section of the gene) in the gene coding for monoamine oxidase A in human beings, leading to a congenital "complete and selective deficiency of enzymatic activity of monoamine oxidase A" has been correlated with "a syndrome of borderline mental retardation and abnormal behavior" including "impulsive aggression, arson, attempted rape and exhibitionism" (MAO-A is one of two types of MAO; harmaline has been shown to inhibit MAO-A) [Brunner *et al.* 1993; McKenna & Towers 1984]. Although medicinal MAO-inhibition has not been correlated with aggression, this congenital, lifelong deficiency of MAO activity decidedly is, although only the males having this genetic defect manifest the congenital MAO-inhibition and the consequent mental impairment and aggression. It seems most likely that in males having this genetic defect, DMT and the other short-acting tryptamines would be active orally, without concomitant administration of MAO-inhibitors. This, definitely, is *endohuasca* or, perhaps more appropriately, *congenihuasca*, and it would also be interesting to conduct dream research with this patient cohort, in the light of Callaway's *endohuasca*/dream vision hypothesis.

While there have long been some attempts to relate psychosis to faulty brain metabolism, and 'though DMT was early implicated in this "indole hypothesis" or "endogenous psychotogen" theory [Ott 1993], solid data have been hard to come by. Here, for the first time, it has been established that a heritable, single point mutation (*i.e.* the alteration of a single base in DNA) leads to biosynthesis of nonfunctional monoamine oxidase enzymes, and consequently to pathological behavior and mental deficiency, apparently as a result of *ayahuasca*-type disordered brain metabolism of neurotransmitters. Paradoxically, psychonautic research on *pharmahuasca* chronicled here, which is so far out of the scientific mainstream that nearly three decades had to pass before unfunded and independent scientists working underground and in secrecy put the enzyme-inhibitor theory of *ayahuasca* pharmacology to the test, may turn out to be at the center of research on the biochemistry of consciousness and the genetics of pathological brain function!

It is also worth noting that a privately-funded group is examining the biochemistry and pharmacology of *ayahuasca* in a group of long-time users in Brazil (members of *União do Vegetal*, see Chapter Four) and comparing them to a group of age-matched controls [McKenna 1993]. One goal of this project is to relate long-term use of *ayahuasca* with known therapeutic indices of MAO-inhibition associated with chronic use of drugs like *Marplan*. Not only is *ayahuasca* research now at the neuroscientific cutting edge, but the reversible MAO-inhibitors in *ayahuasca* may prove to be viable, less toxic alternatives to the noxious compounds currently in use!

DIET AND MAO-INHIBITORS: A SURPRISING *CAVEAT*

As mentioned above, administration of the irreversible MAO-inhibitors used in medicine is accompanied by dietary restrictions. Since these drug diminish the capacity of the brain to metabolize monoamines, it has been found that certain foods, especially those rich in tyramine (4-hydroxy-β-phenethylamine), must be severely restricted in the diet, to avoid toxic interactions involving hypertension, headache, nausea, even intracranial bleeding. Thus tyramine-rich foods such as liver, yeast and fermented foods like cheeses, wines, beers *etc.* must be eliminated from the diet of patients receiving irreversible MAO-inhibitors.

Coincidentally, the anthropological literature on *ayahuasca* shamanism in South America makes reference to several dietary proscriptions enforced on the neophyte *ayahuasquero* [Luna 1984a,1984b]. This diet may consist only of plantains and of certain fish—sugar, salt, *chile* and other spices are usually prohibited, as are meats, eggs and alcohol. Furthermore, sexual continence is an essential feature of training for *ayahuasca*. The fact that dietary restrictions with a pharmacological rationale are an established part of medicinal therapy with MAO-inhibitors, and that dietary restrictions may also be associated with use of *ayahuasca* in Amazonia, a potion now known to contain MAO-inhibitors, has led some researchers to jump to the conclusion that the Amazonian dietary restrictions have a similar pharmacological rationale. However, on examining the list of foods restricted to an *ayahuasquero* in Amazonia, it is clear that this is a specious equivalence—obviously, the Amazonian restrictions are part of a bland "purificatory" diet such as is commonly associated with traditional use of entheogens elsewhere, like the use of psilocybian mushrooms in México [Wasson 1980; Wasson & Wasson 1957]. The collateral restriction of sexual activity, such as occurs also with mushroom use in México, emphasizes that the Amazonian restrictions are motivated by *spiritual*, not pharmacological concerns. The reversible MAO-inhibitors from *ayahuasca* have different substrate specificity than the irreversible medicinal MAO-inhibitors, greatly different pharmacokinetics [McKenna & Towers 1984] and are a great deal less toxic. Indeed, in the aftermath of several of my *ayahuasca* analogue experiments, I have intentionally dined on cheese sandwiches washed down with beer and chased with chocolate (a potentially-rich source of β-phenethylamine; Ott 1985), with absolutely no ill effects. It is probable that the transient MAO-inhibition of the β-carbolines in *ayahuasca* has ceased or greatly diminished by the time the DMT effects are over, but prudence would dictate not ingesting cheese, beer and chocolate *during* the trip! Generally, short-term fasting is a good idea before taking *ayahuasca* or any other entheogen. Not only do these drugs effect nausea in some patients, but the fulsome feeling of a stuffed belly is not conducive, shall we say, to a "higher *chakra* experience." This *spiritual* factor explains the dietary restrictions associated with *ayahuasca* and many other traditional entheogens, which is quite unrelated to the coincidental dietary restrictions associated with medicinal MAO-inhibitors. After all, in the case of *ayahuasca*, one is *seeking* exactly the disordered monoamine metabolism with respect to DMT that the restriction of tyramine in the diet is designed to *prevent*, and we mustn't forget that occasional euphoric reactions to medicinal MAO-inhibitors are regarded to be a *negative* side-effect of the therapy!

The unexpected *caveat* is not that phenethylamines in *ayahuasca* are dangerous; we know this is not the case. The *caveat* here is to be very careful not to go beyond the data and jump to conclusions. This applies also to the data on *ayahuasca* and *pharmahuasca* presented in this book. We have only 25 data points on chemistry of *ayahuasca* lianas; only 15 on *ayahuasca* leaf admixtures; only 16 analyses of *ayahuasca* potions. As for *pharmahuasca*, we have only some three dozen data points involving a small handful of psychonauts. I have milked these data for all they are worth, but am acutely aware of their limitations. *Extreme caution* is advisable with regard to psychonautic experimentation... look before you leap, and don't make facile assumptions based on superficial understanding from limited and fragmentary data! If you are in doubt... don't jump in at all... leave it to the experts! *Caveat emptor*!

CHAPTER FOUR
From Pan–Amazonian to Pan–Gæan Entheogen

The first written mention of *ayahuasca* appears to have been by Jesuit priest José Chantre y Herrera [1901], who at the end of the seventeenth century alluded to a *brebaje diabólico* (diabolical potion) made of *ayahuasca* lianas by the Indians of the Mainas district, in the upper Amazon area of Perú. Some years later, another Jesuit, J. Magnin, made a similar observation in the same area [Magnin 1740], and in 1737 a Jesuit priest named Maroni gave more details about "an intoxicating potion ingested for divinatory and other purposes and called *ayahuasca*, which deprives one of his senses and, at times, of his life" [Jiménez de la Espada 1889]. On the other hand, later naturalist/explorers like C.M. de la Condamine, F.H.A. von Humboldt and C.F.P. von Martius all failed to mention the "diabolical potion" [Reichel-Dolmatoff 1975; Schultes 1986b]. As outlined in Chapter One, it remained for the pioneering British botanist Richard Spruce to initiate scientific studies of the *ayahuasca* complex in 1851–1859, and the first scientist or outsider to experience the full effects of the potion appears to have been Ecuadorian geographer Manuel Villavicencio in the upper Río Napo region in 1858 [Spruce 1873; Villavicencio 1858]. Archæological remains in South America testify to the antiquity of *ayahuasca* use [Naranjo 1986]. In this final chapter, we shall examine the story of *ayahuasca's* astonishing transformation from an ancient, pan-Amazonian ethnomedicine into a much-esteemed, modern, worldwide or pan-Gæan entheogen.

The publication by R. Zerda Bayón [1915] of his notes on travel in Amazonian Colombia made references to the alleged telepathic effects of *ayahuasca*, and to the early chemical work by this author and G. Fischer Cárdenas who, having isolated harmine from the drug and mistakenly believing it to be a novel compound, named the compound *telepatina* or telepathine. This inspired the famous American writer William S. Burroughs to journey to Colombia in 1953 in search of what he called his "final fix." Burroughs experienced *ayahuasca* first-hand and made experiments with *Banisteriopsis* material he collected. In 1963, he published a book of his letters to poet Allen Ginsberg, as well as Ginsberg's letter to Burroughs from Perú in 1960, describing his own *ayahuasca* experience [Burroughs & Ginsberg 1963]. *The Yage Letters* were to influence greatly modern consciousness of the Amazonian *amrta*, and to disseminate the idea of the telepathic properties of the drug, 'though neither Burroughs nor Ginsberg had reported anything like a telepathic experience.

Eight years later, an obscure mestizo *ayahuasquero* named Manuel Córdova-Ríos and F. Bruce Lamb published *Wizard* [sic] *of the Upper Amazon*, an account of the purported boyhood abduction of Córdova-Ríos by Amahuaca Indians, and his subsequent grooming as their chief, including the use of *ayahuasca* that allegedly provoked shared group visions, a poor man's telepathy [Córdova-Ríos & Lamb 1971]. While looking for a publisher, Lamb had sent the manuscript to Amahuaca expert R.L. Carneiro, who told him that Córdova-Ríos' tale was "an imaginative piece of jungle fiction" and who later recommended that Natural History Press reject the manuscript when they sent it to him for evaluation, which that press did [Carneiro 1980]. Atheneum published *Wizard*, and when the American writer A.T. Weil cited it in his best-selling first book *The Natural Mind* [Weil 1972], it gained prominence. Weil did not know Carneiro had denounced the book as fictitious, and accepted it at face value, as ethnography, citing the accounts of *ayahuasca* sessions as evidence of what he called "the reality of shared consciousness." Weil even wrote a laudatory introduction to a second edition of the book [Lamb 1974], again referring to the supposititious telepathic powers of *ayahuasca*, and the book was later reprinted as "Ethnomedicine," with a *verso* quotation about "group vision sessions" from Weil's introduction, accompanied by another *verso* quotation describing "*communal* visions" [emphasis in the original] from *ayahuasca*. Lamb even milked the interest in alleged "telepathic" *ayahuasca* for a sequel, *Río Tigre and Beyond*.

Astonished by the success of what he regarded to be "jungle fiction" tricked up as ethnography, Carneiro decided "to lift the mask of respectability and reveal the imposture," and published an essay explaining numerous errors and incongruities in the tale which led him to call it *Chimera of the Upper Amazon* (Córdova-Ríos had assigned to the little-known Amahuaca composite traits gleaned from superficial observation of various Amazonian Indian groups, particularly the Bora and Witoto) [Carneiro 1980]. By the time this *exposé* appeared, Córdova-Ríos was dead, after enjoying fame and success brought him by the book. Nevertheless, Carneiro quoted Córdova-Ríos admonishing people overawed by his colorful tales: "Don't believe everything I tell you. It could all be a lie." (*No crean todo lo que les digo. Puede ser todo mentira*.) Nonetheless, Lamb challenged Carneiro's opinion (despite having

Table IV-A
Plants Containing MAO-Inhibiting β-Carbolines*

AGARICACEAE
Coriolus maximus (Mont.) Murrill [Harman[1]]
APOCYNACEAE
Amsonia tabernaemontana Walt. [Harmine[2] etc.]
Apocynum cannabinum L. [Harmalol]
Ochrosia nakaiana Koidz [Harman]
BIGNONIACEAE
Newbouldia laevis Bentham et Hooker *fil.* [Harman]
CALYCANTHACEAE
Calycanthus occidentalis Hooker et Arnot [Harmine]
CHENOPODIACEAE
Hammada leptoclada (Pop) Iljin [Tetrahydroharman etc.]
Kochia scoparia (L.) Schrader [Harmine etc.]
COMBRETACEAE
Guiera senegalensis Lamarck [Harman etc.]
CYPERACEAE
Carex brevicollis DC. [Harmine etc.]
ELAEAGNACEAE
Elaeagnus angustifolia L. [Harman etc.]
Elaeagnus hortensis M.B. [Tetrahydroharman etc.]
Elaeagnus orientalis L. [Tetrahydroharman]
Elaeagnus spinosa L. [Tetrahydroharman]
Hippophae rhamnoides L. [Harman etc.]
Shepherdia argentea Nuttall [Tetrahydroharmol]
Shepherdia canadensis Nuttall [Tetrahydroharmol]
GRAMINEAE
Arundo donax L. [Tetrahydroharman etc.]
Festuca arundinacea Schreber [Harman etc.]
Lolium perenne L. [Harman etc.]
LEGUMINOSAE
Acacia baileyana F. von Mueller [Tetrahydroharman]
Acacia complanata A. Cunn. [Tetrahydroharman etc.]
Burkea africana Hooker [Harman etc.]
Desmodium pulchellum Bentham ex Baker [Harman etc.]

[73]

Mucuna pruriens DC. [6-Methoxy-Harman]

Petalostylis labicheoides R. Brown [Tetrahydroharman]

Prosopis nigra (Grisebach) Hieronymus [Harman *etc.*]
  LOGANIACEAE

Strychnos usambarensis Gilg. [Harman]
  MALPIGHIACEAE

Banisteriopsis caapi (Spruce ex Grisebach) Morton [Harmine *etc.*]

Banisteriopsis lutea (Grisebach) Cuatrecasas [Harmine]

Banisteriopsis muricata (Cavanilles) Cuatrecasas [Harmine *etc.*]

Callaeum antifebrile (Grisebach) Johnson (=*Cabi paraensis*) [Harmine]
  MYRISTICACEAE

Virola cuspidata (Bentham) Warburg [6-Methoxy-Harman]
  PASSIFLORACEAE

Passiflora actinea Hooker [Harman=Passiflorine]

Passiflora alata Aiton [Harman]

Passiflora alba Link et Otto [Harman]

Passiflora bryonoides Humboldt Bonpland et Kunth [Harman]

Passiflora caerulea L. [Harman]

Passiflora capsularis L. [Harman]

Passiflora decaisneana Nichol [Harman]

Passiflora edulis Sims [Harman]

Passiflora eichleriana Mast. [Harman]

Passiflora foetida L. [Harman]

Passiflora incarnata L. [Harmine, Harmaline,[3] Harman, *etc.*]

Passiflora quadrangularis L. [Harman]

Passiflora aff. *ruberosa* L. [Harman]

Passiflora subpeltata Ortega [Harman]

Passiflora warmingii Mast. [Harman]
  POLYGONACEAE

Calligonum minimum Lipski [Harman *etc.*]
  RUBIACEAE

Leptactinia densiflora Hooker *fil.* [Leptaflorine, *etc.*]

Nauclea diderrichii [Harman *etc.*]

Ophiorrhiza japonica Blume [Harman]

Pauridiantha callicarpoides Bremek [Harman]

Pauridiantha dewevrei Bremek [Harman]

Pauridiantha lyalli Bremek [Harman]

Pauridiantha viridiflora Hepper [Harman]
Simira klugii Standley [Harman]
Simira rubra K. Schumann [Harman]
Uncaria attenuata Korth. [Harman]
Uncaria canescens Korth. [Harman]
Uncaria orientalis Guillemin [Harman]
    SAPOTACEAE
Chrysophyllum lacourtianum De Wild. [Norharman *etc.*]
    SYMPLOCACEAE
Symplocos racemosa Roxburgh [Harman]
    ZYGOPHYLLACEAE
Fagonia cretica L. [Harman]
Peganum harmala L. [Harmaline, Harmine, *etc.*]
Tribulus terrestris L. [Harmine *etc.*]
Zygophyllum fabago L. [Harmine, *etc.*]

NOTES

[1]   Harman (1-methyl-9H-pyrido[3,4-b]indole or 1-methyl-β-carboline) is by far the most widespread MAO-inhibiting β-carboline, having been found in at least 45 species in thirteen families. It is especially common in the Passifloraceae (15 species) and Rubiaceae (11 species), and is also known by the name *passiflorine*. Other less-common synonyms for harman are: *aribine*, *locuturine*, *loturine* and *zygofabagine*. While *in vitro* tests using rat, calf and mouse liver and brain homogenates showed potent MAO-inhibiting effects of harman (see footnote below), a self-experiment by a colleague with 250 mg harman hydrochloride plus 35 mg DMT (a potentially active amount) provoked no effects, suggesting oral harman is inactive as a human MAO-inhibitor.

[2]   Harmine (7-methoxy-1-methyl-9H-pyrido[3,4-b]indole), the major alkaloid of *ayahuasca*, acquired the synonyms *banisterine*, *telepathine* and *yajéine*, and is also known as *leucoharmine*. This compound is only known from eight species in six families outside of the *ayahuasca* complex, including *Peganum harmala* and its relatives in the family Zygophyllaceae, *Tribulus terrestris* and *Zygophyllum fabago*.

[3]   Harmaline (4,9-dihydro-7-methoxy-1-methyl-9H-pyrido[3,4-b]indole; dihydroharmine) is found outside of the *ayahuasca* Malpighiaceae only in *Passiflora incarnata* and *Peganum harmala*. It is unfortunate that this rare compound, unimportant in *ayahuasca* pharmacology, has received so much pharmacological attention at the expense of harmine.

[*]   This table lists plant species containing simple β-carboline alkaloids which are known to

be MAO-inhibitors. Four separate studies have found potent, reversible MAO-inhibiting effects of simple β-carbolines in rat liver homogenates [Udenfriend *et al.* 1958], in calf liver mitochondrial homogenates [McIsaac & Estévez 1966], in mouse brain and liver homogenates [Buckholtz & Boggan 1977] and in rat liver homogenates [McKenna *et al.* 1984a]. Considering the four most important plant-derived compounds—harmine, harmaline, harman and leptaflorine—the Udenfriend group established harmine and harmaline as roughly equipotent, followed by harman and leptaflorine; McIsaac and Estévez found harman to be the most potent (with norharman being more potent still), followed by harmine and harmaline; Buckholtz and Boggan determined that harmaline was slightly more potent than harmine, with harman and leptaflorine less potent; and the McKenna group found harmine and harmaline roughly equipotent, again followed by harman and leptaflorine. As noted in footnote 1 on the preceding page, there is some doubt as to the oral efficacy of harman as a human MAO-inhibitor, about which further research is needed. This table is abstracted from the excellent review "The simple β-carboline alkaloids" [Allen & Holmstedt 1980], which lists a total of 112 species in 27 families containing simple β-carbolines, and the reader is referred to this paper for 228 references to this important branch of phytochemistry. Data on structure-activity relationships with respect to MAO-inhibition provoked by these compounds are summarized in the McKenna paper [1984a]. See structures of harman and related plant β-carbolines below.

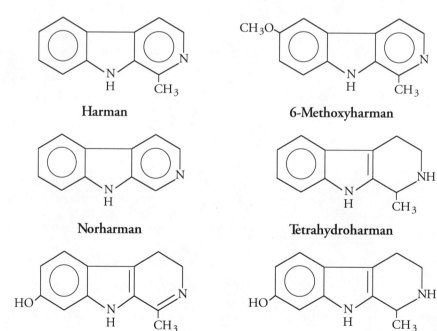

Harman

6-Methoxyharman

Norharman

Tetrahydroharman

Harmalol

Tetrahydroharmol

himself originally sought it), arguing one might extract some kernels of ethnography from Córdova-Ríos' fables [Lamb 1981a,1981b]. More than any other book, this Castanedesque tall tale was to inform modern consciousness of the jungle *ambrosia*.

In 1970 Ecuadorian scientist Plutarco Naranjo published the first full-length book on *ayahuasca*, written in Spanish and later appearing in a revised edition [Naranjo 1983]. Two years later, American anthropologist Marlene Dobkin de Ríos published *The Visionary Vine*, an account of divinatory use of *ayahuasca* among urban mestizos of Perú [Dobkin de Ríos 1972]. Various books by the Colombian scientist Gerardo Reichel-Dolmatoff [1971,1975,1978] further drew scientific attention to *ayahuasca*. Also important in this regard was an obscure book by the *ayahuasca* researcher Dennis J. McKenna and brother Terence K. McKenna, which referred to a sort of *ayahuasca* potion with psilocybian mushrooms as the tryptamine source [McKenna & McKenna 1975]. I might mention also in this regard a critique of colonialism and anthropology by Michael Taussig [1987], which gave considerable space to *ayahuasca*. None of these books, however, had the popular impact of the Córdova-Ríos tale which had been boosted by the attention Weil brought to it. Weil went on to publish a popular article on *ayahuasca* in *High Times*, and incorporated this into a chapter of his second book *The Marriage of the Sun and Moon* [Weil 1980]. Weil described finally sampling the potion in Colombia, and admitted he failed to experience "any telepathic news bulletins of distant events." This admission was too little, too late, and by this time the supposititious "telepathic" drug was famous.

SANTO DAIME AND THE UNIÃO DO VEGETAL

Well before the entheogenic "counterculture" began to rediscover the Amazonian *amrta*, the potion had found a niche in the modern world. Mestizo *ayahuasqueros*, after abandoning their jungle homes for the city, continued to practice *ayahuasca* divinatory healing in urban areas of Perú (like Iquitos and Lima) [Córdova-Ríos & Lamb 1971; Dobkin de Ríos 1972,1973,1992; Lamb 1974] and in the Colombian capital of Bogotá [Ramírez de Jara & Pinzón C. 1986], even as their Indian relatives communed, in ever-decreasing measure, with *Sacha Runa* (the "jungle man") and other "plant spirits" in ever-diminishing islands of primary rainforest throughout Amazonia. Such use has even expanded to other Latin American cities like México City, well beyond the traditional range of shamanic use of *ayahuasca* [Ott 1993].

Perhaps more significant is the contemporary syncretism of *ayahuasca* cults with Christian churches, like *Santo Daime* and the *União do Vegetal* (pronounced "oohnyow due vezh-eh-**taow**"), which started in Acre, Amazonian Brazil, in the 1920s. Raimundo Irineu Serra (1872–1971) had been exposed to Indians who used *ayahuasca* during the 1930s, while he worked as a rubber tapper and an official of the Brazilian agency demarcating the border with Perú. He met two brothers, Antonio and André Costa, who had been initiated into the use of *ayahuasca* by Peruvian shaman Don Cresêncio Pizango and later founded a church called Círculo de Regeneração e Fé (CRF) in the 1920s. These brothers introduced Irineu to *ayahuasca*, and their defunct church is considered to be the precursor of the modern *ayahuasca* churches. Mestre Irineu (as he was known to his disciples) founded his own *ayahuasca* church around 1940, called the Centro de Iluminação Cristã Luz Universal (CICLU), also known as "Alto Santo," in the Acre town of Río Branco. He began to call *ayahuasca* "*Daime*" from invocations like "Dá-me amor, luz, força" ("give me love, light, power"). In his *Santo Daime* religion (the name might be translated as "Saint Gi'me"), *ayahuasca* or *Daime* is the solar, masculine aspect; Nossa Senhora da Conceição or Rainha da Floresta is the lunar, feminine aspect, symbolized by *chacrona*, the tryptamine-rich *Psychotria viridis* leaf added to the potions.

One of Mestre Irineu's disciples, Sebastião Mota de Melo, who became a disciple at Alto Santo in 1965 when Mestre Irineu cured him of a liver ailment, started his own sect of the cult at his ranch Colonia 5000 near Río Branco, where Mestre Irineu authorized him to produce *Daime* and *chacrona* with the understanding that half the production go to Alto Santo. When the two groups split over political differences, the Colonia 5000 branch began to introduce *Cannabis* (*maconha* or *Santa María*) and other entheogens into the liturgy. This provoked a police raid in October 1981, temporarily putting Colonia 5000 out of commission and leading to the illegalization of *ayahuasca* in Brazil in 1985. In January 1983, Padrinho Sebastião and his group moved further into the forest away from the road, and started a new colony called Céu do Mapiá on a tributary of the Río Purús, politicly abandoning the use of *Cannabis*. By 1982, the first urban branch of *Santo Daime* was founded in Río de Janeiro, the Chamou-se Centro Ecléctico Fluente Luz Universal Sebastião Mota de Melo (CEFLUSME), called Céu do Mar for short [MacRae 1992].

Meanwhile, there arose an independent *ayahuasca* church called the Centro Espírita Beneficente União do Vegetal (UDV), founded on 22 July 1961 by José Gabriel da Costa, also in Acre state [Centro 1989; Henman 1986]. This soon became primarily an urban church, which moved its headquarters to Brasilia in the 1970s. Today it is the largest *ayahuasca* church in Brazil, with more than 7000 members. There are other *ayahuasca*-using churches in Brazil, such as the Centro Espírita Culto de Oração Casa de Jesus Fonte de Luz (later called Centro Espírita Daniel

Pereira de Matos), the Centro Ecléctico de Correntes da Luz Universal (CECLU) and Centro Espírita Fé, Luz, Amor e Caridade, all derivatives of Alto Santo and all from Acre state. In May of 1989, a meeting of the *Santo Daime* groups at Céu do Mapiá led to the establishment of a central *Daime* church, the Centro Ecléctico de Fluente Luz Universal Raimundo Irineu Serra (CEFLURIS), with the late Padrinho Sebastião as head [MacRae 1992].

In 1985 the Brazilian Divisão de Medicamentos do Ministério da Saúde (or Dimed) and Conselho Federal de Entorpecentes (Confen) added *Banisteriopsis caapi* to the controlled substances list. The UDV petitioned the government to annul the ban, and a commission was appointed to study the issue. After two years of field work among urban and rural UDV and *Daime* groups, during which ritual use of the sacrament was observed and commission members *themselves* tried it, the commission recommended overturning the ban! No evidence of social disruption was observed, and the ethical and laboral behavior of church members was exemplary. Accordingly, in 1987 *ayahuasca* was removed from the controlled substances list. A year later there occurred an anonymous denunciation of the *ayahuasca* churches to Confen in Río de Janeiro. The preposterous complaint alleged there were 10 million "fanatics" of the sects, the bulk of whom were "toxicomaniacs or ex-guerrillas" (we get a notion of the right-wing political origin of the complaint), given to smoking *Cannabis* and taking LSD during the rites. Confen once again appointed a commission to study the issue, and the *ayahuasca* churches again received a clean bill of health. Not only did the second commission reaffirm the 1987 decree legalizing sacramental *ayahuasca* in Brazil, but it recommended permanent exemption of *ayahuasca* from Brazilian controlled substances laws [MacRae 1992].

This is the state of affairs today in Brazil, where *ayahuasca* churches continue to grow and prosper. In weekly mass, *ayahuasca* is dispensed *in lieu* of the Eucharist from a sort of "Fount of Wisdom," and in *Santo Daime* groups singing and dancing may follow. In the *Santo Daime* liturgy, those communicants most heavily affected by the potion are taken into a back room, where church "Mestres" have their own altars, for individual counseling and ministry. Plantations of *Banisteriopsis caapi* and *Psychotria viridis* have been established in Amazonia to supply urban groups with ingredients for the potion, the large-scale preparation of which is supervised by church officials [McKenna 1992]. Large quantities of *ayahuasca* (hundreds of liters) may be stored on the premises of the churches [Lowy 1987]. It is expressly forbidden to sell the potion, which the *Santo Daime* members call *Daime* and which the UDV members call *Chá Hoasca* [Centro 1989]. Nevertheless, there is some proselytization of the faith, especially by *Santo Daime* enthusiasts. There has lately been celebration of introductory *ayahuasca* sessions in Spain, Catalunya, and other European countries. For a modest "donation" to the church, curious would-be members are allowed to participate in the *ayahuasca* liturgy. Surely this is bending the proscription against selling *ayahuasca*! Attempts by *Santo Daime* proselytes to spiritually edify Americans have thus far been frustrated, and there is at least one case in which U.S. Customs seized and destroyed quantities of the sacrament, on attempts to import it into the United States. Nevertheless, there is at least one "underground" chapter of the *União do Vegetal* now in the United States, and the potential for expansion of these churches in the U.S. is virtually limitless. Unfortunately, this is a country in which freedom of religion is much talked about and seldom allowed! Indeed, the U.S. Constitution doesn't separate church and state; it merely separates church from the *federal* state, reserving religious meddling to state governments. Despite the fact that 23 states exempt sacramental use of *péyotl* from controlled substances laws, and a 1979 federal court decision established that sacramental use of *péyotl* cannot be restricted solely to Indians, the U.S. Supreme Court has consistently shirked its responsibility to establish some uniform judicial policy toward minority religions employing *genuine*, and not *placebo* sacraments.[20]

AYAHUASCA ANALOGUES AS PAN-GÆAN ENTHEOGENS

Running in parallel with long-term expansion of *ayahuasca* use in South America, has been an ever-increasing interest in *ayahuasca* among members of the "counter-culture," stimulated by the popular publications outlined above. There has been an unfortunate trend toward *ayahuasca* tourism, which commenced at least as early as 1980—transportation of tour groups to Amazonia with the implicit purpose of obtaining *ayahuasca* [Ott 1993]. This is attracting the wrong kind of attention to the Amazonian *amrta*, and contributing to the accelerated decrescence of shamanic usage of *ayahuasca* by turning the potion into a tourist commodity. Mushroomic tourism in México in the 1970s contributed to the premature demise of shamanic use of *teonanácatl* [Ott 1975], and a similar phenomenon is occurring today in México with regard to *péyotl* [Valadez 1986]. Whereas popular dissemination of information on cultivation of psilocybian mushrooms and identification of non-Mexican species helped diffuse mushroomic tourism [Ott 1993], the possibility of making *ayahuasca* analogues is having a similar effect on *ayahuasca* tourism. The present book is designed to encourage and foment this welcome trend.

As my analogue experiments amply demonstrate, the readily-available and legal

[80]

TABLE IV-B
PLANTS CONTAINING ENTHEOGENIC TRYPTAMINES*

ACANTHACEAE

Justicia pectoralis Jac. var. *stenophylla* Lnd.[1] [DMT,l] [Schultes&Holmstedt 1968]

AGARICACEAE

Amanita citrina Gray[2] [DMT,5MD,w] [Tyler & Gröger 1964]

Amanita porphyria (Fries) Secretan[2] [5MD,w] [Tyler & Gröger 1964]

AIZOACEAE

Delosperma sp.[3] [DMT] [Deulofeu 1973; Rivier & Pilet 1971]

GRAMINEAE

Arundo donax L.[2] [DMT,l,r,f] [Ghosal *et al.* 1969; Ghosal *et al.* 1972d]

Phalaris arundinacea L. [DMT,5MD,l,w] [Barnes *et al.* 1971; Culvenor *et al.* 1964; Gander *et al.* 1976; Marten *et al.* 1973; Williams *et al.* 1971]

Phalaris tuberosa L. (=*P. aquatica*)[DMT,5MD,l] [Culvenor *et al.* 1964; Baxter & Slaytor 1972; Frahn & Illman 1973; Moore *et al.* 1967; Mulvena & Slaytor 1982; Oram & Williams 1967]

Phragmites australis (Cav.) Trin. ex Steud. [DMT,r] [Wassel *et al.* 1985]

LEGUMINOSAE

Acacia confusa Merr.[2] [DMT,st] [Arthur *et al.* 1967]

Acacia maidenii F. von Mueller [DMT,b] [Fitzgerald & Sioumis 1965]

Acacia nubica Bentham[2] [DMT,l] [Wahba Khalil & Elkheir 1975]

Acacia phlebophylla F. von Mueller [DMT,l] [Rovelli & Vaughan 1967]

Acacia polyacantha Willdenow subsp. *campylacantha*[2] Hochst. ex A. Rich [DMT,l] [Wahba Khalil & Elkheir 1975]

Acacia senegal (L.) Willdenow[2] [DMT,l] [Wahba Khalil & Elkheir 1975]

Acacia simplicifolia Druce [DMT,b,l,st] [Poupat *et al.* 1976]

Anadenanthera colubrina (Vellozo) Brennan var. *cébil* (Grisebach) Altschul (=*Piptadenia macrocarpa*) [DMT,s,p] [Fish *et al.* 1955]

Anadenanthera excelsa Grisebach [DMT,s,p] [Iacobucci & Rúveda 1964]

Anadenanthera peregrina (L.) Spegazzini [DMT,5MD,b,l,s,p] [Agurell *et al.* 1969; Fish *et al.* 1955; Legler & Tschesche 1963]

Desmanthus illinoensis (Michx.) MacM. [DMT,r,rb] [Thompson *et al.* 1987]

Desmodium caudatum DC. [DMT,r,st] [Ueno *et al.* 1978]

Desmodium gangeticum DC. [DMT,5MD,w,r,st,l] [Banerjee & Ghosal 1969; Ghosal & Banerjee 1969; Ghosal & Bhattacharya 1972]

Desmodium gyrans DC.[2] [DMT,5MD,l,r] [Ghosal *et al.* 1972c]

Desmodium pulchellum Bentham ex Baker [DMT,5MD,w,r,st,l,f] [Ghosal &
Mukherjee 1964,1965,1966; Ghosal *et al.* 1972a]

Desmodium racemosum Thunberg [5MD,w] [Hsu 1970]

Desmodium triflorum DC.[2] [DMT-*N*-oxide,r] [Ghosal *et al.* 1971a,1972b]

Lespedeza bicolor Turczaninow var. *japonica* Nakai [DMT,5MD,l,rb] [Gotu *et
al.* 1958; Morimoto & Matsumoto 1966; Morimoto & Oshio 1965]

Mimosa hostilis Benth.[4] [DMT,r] [Gonçalves de Lima 1946; Pachter *et al.* 1959]

Mimosa scabrella Bentham [DMT,b] [De Moraes *et al.* 1990]

Mimosa tenuiflora (Willd.) Poir. [DMT,5MD,b] [Meckes-Lozoya *et al.* 1990]

Mucuna pruriens DC. [DMT,5MD,l,s,st,r] [Bhattacharya *et al.* 1971; Ghosal
1972; Ghosal *et al.* 1971b]

Petalostylis labicheoides R. Br. var. *casseoides* Benth. [DMT,l,st] [Johns *et al.* 1966]

MALPIGHIACEAE

Banisteriopsis muricata (Cavanilles) Cuatrecasas[2] (=*B. argentea*) [DMT,st,l]
[Ghosal & Mazumder 1971; Ghosal *et al.* 1971c]

Diplopterys cabrerana (Cuatrecasas) Gates (=*Banisteriopsis rusbyana*)
[DMT,5MD,l] [Agurell *et al.* 1968; Der Marderosian *et al.* 1968; McKenna
et al. 1984a; Poisson 1965]

MYRISTICACEAE

Iryanthera ulei Warburg[2] [5MD,b] [Holmstedt *et al.* 1980]

Osteophloem platyspermum (DC.) Warb.[5] [DMT,5MD,b] [Holmstedt *et al.* 1980]

Virola calophylla Warburg [DMT,5MD,b,r,l,s,f] [Agurell *et al.* 1969; Holmstedt
et al. 1980; McKenna *et al.* 1984b]

Virola calophylloidea Markgraf [DMT,5MD,b,l] [Holmstedt *et al.* 1980]

Virola carinata (Spruce ex Bentham) Warburg[2] [DMT,l] [Holmstedt *et al.* 1980]

Virola divergens Ducke[2] [DMT,l] [Holmstedt *et al.* 1980]

Virola elongata (Spruce ex Bentham) Warburg[2] [DMT,5MD,b,l] [Holmstedt
et al. 1980; McKenna *et al.* 1984b]

Virola melinonii (Benoist) A.C. Smith[2] [DMT,b] [Holmstedt *et al.* 1980]

Virola multinervia Ducke[2] [DMT,5MD,b,r] [Agurell *et al.* 1969; Holmstedt *et
al.* 1980]

Virola pavonis (DC.) Smith [DMT,l] [McKenna *et al.* 1984b]

Virola peruviana (DC.) Warburg [DMT,5MD,b] [Holmstedt *et al.* 1980]

Virola rufula (DC.) War. [DMT,5MD,b,r,l] [Agurell *et al.* 1969; Holmstedt *et al.* 1980]

Virola sebifera Aublet [DMT,b] [Corothie & Nakano 1969]

Virola theiodora (Spruce ex Bentham) Warburg [DMT,5MD,b,r,l,f] [Agurell *et
al.* 1969; Holmstedt *et al.* 1980]

Virola venosa (Bentham) Warburg[2] [DMT,5MD,r,l] [Agurell *et al.* 1969; Holmstedt *et al.* 1980]
OCHNACEAE
Testulea gabonensis Pellegr. [DMT,b,rb] [Leboeuf *et al.* 1977]
POLYGONACEAE
Erigonum sp. [DMT] [Schroeder 1986]
RUBIACEAE
Psychotria carthaginensis Jacquin [DMT,l] [Rivier & Lindgren 1972]
Psychotria viridis Ruíz et Pavón (=*P. psychotriaefolia*)[DMT,l] [Der Marderosian *et al.* 1970; McKenna *et al.* 1984a; Rivier & Lindgren 1972]
RUTACEAE
Dictyoloma incanescens DC. [5MD,b] [Pachter *et al.* 1959]
Dutaillyea drupacea (Baillon) Hartley [5MD,l] [Baudouin *et al.* 1981]
Dutaillyea oreophila (Baillon) Sévenet-Pusset [5MD,l] [Baudouin *et al.* 1981]
Evodia rutaecarpa Bentham [5MD,fr] [Takagi *et al.* 1979]
Limonia acidissima L.[2] [DMT,st] [Abu Zarga 1986]
Melicope leptococca (Baillon) Guillaumin [5MD,l,st] [Skaltsounis *et al.* 1983]
Pilocarpus organensis Rizzini et Occhioni [5MD,l] [Balsam & Voigtländer 1978]
Vepris ampody H. Perr. [DMT,l] [Kan-Fan *et al.* 1970]
Zanthoxylum arborescens Rose[6] [DMT,l] [Grina *et al.* 1982]
Zanthoxylum procerum Donn. Sm. [DMT,l] [Schroeder 1986]

NOTES

[1] Although preliminary tests indicated the presence of DMT in this aromatic additive to entheogenic *Virola* snuffs used by some Waiká Indians [Schultes & Holmstedt 1968], subsequent tests failed to confirm this [McKenna *et al.* 1984b]. The plant may be used simply to flavor or preserve the snuffs. On the other hand, the McKenna group found DMT and 5-MeO-DMT in a botanically-undocumented Yanomamö snuff sample from Venezuela, *mashahari*, evidently prepared exclusively from *Justicia pectoralis*. The authors noted the anomaly, and speculated that there might have been an unknown additive, or a tryptamine-rich chemical race of *Justicia pectoralis*.

[2] These species contain trace amounts of entheogenic tryptamines (*i.e.* below 0.02%), and are probably unsuitable for use in *ayahuasca* analogues.

[3] I have been unable to locate the primary report of tryptamines in the *Delosperma* species [Deulofeu 1973]. As this is widely cited in secondary reports, I include this species here.

[4] In preliminary chemical study of *Mimosa hostilis* root used as the basis of the Brazilian

enthogenic potion *vinho de jurema*, an alkaloid named *nigerina* or nigerine was isolated [Gonçalves de Lima 1946]. Thirteen years later DMT was isolated in good yield at the Smith, Kline and French pharmaceutical laboratories in the United States from roots of *Mimosa hostilis* provided by Gonçalves de Lima, and it is widely thought that *nigerina* was in fact DMT [Pachter *et al.* 1959]. Although *M. nigra* and *M. verrucosa* were reported by Gonçalves de Lima as alternate bases for potions, these remain unstudied chemically.

5 When Holmstedt's group conducted extensive chemical analyses of myristicaceous snuff plants during the Alpha Helix Amazon Expedition of 1977, they reported enthogenic tryptamines in many species of *Virola*, in *Iryanthera ulei*, and in *Osteophloem platyspermum* [Holmstedt *et al.* 1980]. The name of the latter was written in a table as *O. platyphyllum* [*nomen nudum*], although it was correctly spelled in an appendix. Analysis of a single sample of leaves of this plant detected only *N*-methyltryptophan methyl ester [McKenna *et al.* 1984b]; in this paper, alas, the name was incorrectly spelled in the table as *O. platysperumum*. Sap of this species is used by Quijos Quichua Indians as an oral enthogen in combination with a *Brugmansia* species and *Tabernaemontana sananho* [Alarcón 1990].

6 *Zanthoxylum martinicense* of the Caribbean is said to be "narcotic" and is used as an ingredient in the Haitian *zombi* poison [Davis 1988], and may also be a source of tryptamines. Bark of a *Zanthoxylum* species is used as a topical analgesic by Amazonian Kofán Indians [Schultes & Raffauf 1990], and similar use is made of bark infusions of a North American *Zanthoxylum* species known colloquially as the "toothache tree."

* See also the review by T.A. Smith [1977], which lists 92 species or genera containing one or several of 19 tryptamines, with a bibliography of 119 sources. Letters in square brackets refer to DMT and 5-MeO-DMT [5MD] in leaves [l], seeds [s], pods [p], stems [st], bark [b], roots [r], flowers [f], fruit [fr], root bark [rb] or whole plant [w]. Excluded is the report of DMT in *Prestonia amazonica* [Hochstein & Paradies 1957], (see Note 17 and Schultes & Raffauf 1960). This is the only report of tryptamines of any kind in the family Apocynaceae, which is a rich source of species containing indole alkaloids of the ibogaine series [Ott 1993; Van Beek *et al.* 1984]. Also excluded are animal species, such as the toad *Bufo alvarius*, whose venom contains 5-MeO-DMT, since the literature in this area is rudimentary. The evidence indicates that virtually *all* mammalian species will be found to contain DMT, probably a mammalian neurotransmitter. Any attempt to list animal species possessing DMT, a list which would include *Homo sapiens*, would be hopelessly selective and inadequate. See *Pharmacotheon* for references to this incipient field [Ott 1993].

N,*N*-Dimethyltryptamine   5-Methoxy-*N*,*N*-Dimethyltryptamine

Peganum harmala or Syrian rue seeds can efficiently and safely replace *Banisteriopsis* species as a source of the MAO-inhibiting β-carbolines. Indeed, these seeds contain roughly ten times the concentrations of β-carbolines found in *Banisteriopsis* stems. They are used to dye textiles and as incense, and are easily and cheaply available from Middle Eastern groceries, under the Arabic name *esphand*, for approximately $25–30 *per* kilogram. Table IV-A lists 67 species of plants which contain known MAO-inhibiting β-carbolines, some of which might also be useful in formulating *ayahuasca* analogues. The reader is also referred to the excellent review by Holmstedt and Allen [1980], which lists 112 species in 27 families known as of 1980 to contain β-carboline alkaloids, and features an excellent bibliography to this literature.

Table IV-B lists 62 species of plants reported to contain either DMT or 5-MeO-DMT, with indications as to the appropriate plant parts. Not all of these species are suitable for *ayahuasca* analogues—fifteen were reported to contain only traces of entheogenic tryptamines, and for some (*e.g. Justicia pectoralis* var. *stenophylla* and *Psychotria carthaginensis*), there is contradictory evidence. On the other hand, the following ten species have been reported to contain substantial quantities of entheogenic tryptamines: 1) *Phalaris tuberosa*, one Italian strain of which has been said to contain higher levels of DMT than are known from any other species [Samorini 1992]; 2) *Acacia maidenii*, the bark of which contains 0.36% DMT [Fitzgerald & Sioumis 1965]; 3) *Acacia phlebophylla*, whose leaves contain 0.3% DMT [Rovelli & Vaughan 1967]; 4) *Acacia simplicifolia*, reported to contain 0.81% DMT in the bark [Poupat *et al.* 1976]; 5) *Desmanthus illinoensis*, found to have 0.34% DMT in the root bark [Thompson *et al.* 1987]; 6) *Mimosa hostilis*, shown to contain 0.57% DMT in the roots [Pachter *et al.* 1959]; 7) *Virola theiodora*, reported to contain 0.44% DMT in the flowers [Holmstedt *et al.* 1980]; 8) *Melicope leptococca*, with 0.21% 5-MeO-DMT in the leafy branches [Skaltsounis *et al.* 1983]; 9) *Pilocarpus organensis*, having 1.06% alkaloids, chiefly 5-MeO-DMT [Balsam & Voigtländer 1978] and lastly, 10) *Vepris ampody*, shown to contain 0.22% DMT in the leafy branches [Kan-Fan *et al.* 1970].

Potential experimenters are warned of several *caveats*. First and foremost, there is relatively little data on any given plant, and we must not put too much faith in solitary reports. Strain and habitat differences may drastically influence alkaloid concentrations within a given species. Moreover, many of these plants contain other alkaloids or phytotoxins of different chemical categories, apart from the tryptamines. The inactive *N*-methyltryptamine (MMT) often accompanies DMT and/or 5-MeO-DMT in plants (for example in *D. illinoensis* roots, of which 25% of the tryptamine fraction is MMT), which poses no problems, but the noxious bufotenine

(5-OH-DMT) is found in some plants, like *Anadenanthera* spp. [Fish *et al.* 1955; Pachter *et al.* 1959]. Some species contain other alkaloids of known toxicity, for example the psychoactive *péyotl* alkaloid hordenine in *Desmodium gangeticum* and *Dutaillyea oreophila* [Baudouin *et al.* 1981; Ghosal & Banerjee 1969]. Worse still, numerous known and novel alkaloids of obscure toxicity have been found in some of these plants, like *Melicope leptococca*, which contained eight alkaloids apart from 5-MeO-DMT and its *N*-oxide [Skaltsounis *et al.* 1983], and *Vepris ampody*, with seven alkaloids apart from DMT [Kan-Fan *et al.* 1970].[21] Most dangerous of all is the possibility that some tryptamine-containing species might also harbor highly toxic compounds yet undiscovered. What if, for example, it were to turn out that *Pilocarpus organensis* contained the highly toxic imidazole alkaloid pilocarpine, already known from several species of the genus? Or what if a friendly neighborhood herb dealer mistook a toxic *Pilocarpus* for *P. organensis*? The would-be discoverer of a novel *ayahuasca* analogue just might become an inadvertent discoverer of a new deadly-poisonous plant! Before ingesting *any* plant or "herb" do your homework, consult the literature, make certain that there is at least some track-record for human ingestion of the plant, which can give guidelines as to potential toxicity and dosage. Look before you leap; use your head before blindly ingesting *any* unfamiliar plant, for any reason! I cannot emphasize this too strongly... this is a dangerous business, and casualties are all-too-possible. My advice is... if in doubt, *don't do it*!

On the other hand, in time and with careful experimentation, we are certain to discover additional safe and effective tryptamine sources for *ayahuasca* analogues. We already know *Acacia phlebophylla* and *Desmanthus illinoensis* are suitable, and I think it probable that *Acacia simplicifolia*, *Acacia maidenii*, *Phalaris tuberosa* and possibly some of the rutaceous species will prove to be safe and effective sources of tryptamines for *ayahuasca* analogues. Computer bulletin boards like *Alt.Drugs* on the *Internet* are excellent fora for exchanging information on psychonautic experiments, but *Cave Fratem*... beware that *Big Brother* is listening, too [Levy 1991; Sterling 1992]! The marked advantage of *ayahuasca* analogues over other entheogens, like LSD, mescaline or psilocybian mushrooms, is that even city apartment dwellers, with no land or chemical or botanical knowledge, and not needing the long-term commitment of time and energy required to master tricky procedures like cultivation of entheogenic mushrooms, can theoretically prepare a safe and effective entheogen in less than half an hour, using technology and equipment already available for making caffeine-enriched extracts of coffee beans! Furthermore, rather than run risks by having to purchase and use watched chemicals or equipment, simple dried herbs, some of which are already available commercially and have various licit uses unrelated to *ayahuasca* analogues, can be instantly transformed into entheogenic potions with water, lemon juice and heat, with no danger whatever to the consumer! The cosmopolitan nature of potential source plants for *ayahuasca* analogues is another distinct advantage—no smuggling required! *Ayahuasca borealis* can be made, after all, from *Peganum harmala* seeds and *Desmanthus illinoensis* roots, northern shrubs from semi-arid climates; ecologically and morphologically as different as can be from the rain-forest lianas used to make *ayahuasca australis*! We have here indeed, the potential for a pan-Gæan entheogen for the new millennium!

EPILOGUE: A *PANACÆA* FOR *PANGÆA*?

Exactly two hundred years ago, on 10 October 1793, a 35-year-old London engraver offered for sale productions of ten of his own "illuminated" works: "of equal magnitude and consequence with the productions of any age" including, for the price of 7 shillings 6 pence, a remarkable "Prophetic Book" with 14 illustrations entitled *The Marriage of Heaven and Hell*. If anything, William Blake was guilty of understatement, for this wide-ranging satire of politics, religion and philosophy is nothing less than one of the greatest poems ever penned, in English or any other language. Appalled by the spiritual materialism of his contemporaries, and haunted by the spectre of the Industrial Revolution then casting its long shadow over England, Blake's poetic words are as meaningful and actual today as two centuries ago:

> All Bibles or sacred codes have been the causes of the following Errors: 1. That Man has two real existing principles: Viz: a Body & a Soul. 2. That Energy, call'd Evil, is alone from the Body; & that Reason, call'd Good, is alone from the Soul. 3. That God will torment Man in Eternity for following his Energies. But the following Contraries to these are True: 1. Man has no Body distinct from his Soul; for that call'd Body is a portion of Soul discern'd by the five Senses, the chief inlets of Soul in this age. 2. Energy is the only life, and is from the Body; and Reason is the bound or outward circumference of Energy. 3. Energy is Eternal Delight.

Blake spoke directly from the *logos*, casting in English words and engraved designs what he saw... nothing seen with his "mortal and perishing" eye, but "organized and minutely articulated" visions perceived by his "imaginative and immortal organs"

[87]

and "in stronger and better light than his perishing eye" could see. Blake saw that there was no conflict berween Flesh and Spirit, Body and Soul; that it was a question rather of a dynamic interplay between matter and energy; that the materialistic perception of solid bodies was but a crude distortion of the all-encompassing reality as filtered through the five senses, "the chief inlets of Soul" in a materialistic age. Recall that to Blake the five senses *closed* humankind to the "immense world of delight" that is "ev'ry Bird that cuts the airy way" [Blake 1946]. Again, Blake:

> But first the notion that man has a body distinct from his soul is
> to be expunged; this I shall do by… melting apparent surfaces
> away, and displaying the infinite which was hid. If the doors of
> perception were cleansed every thing would appear to man as it is,
> infinite. For man has closed himself up, till he sees all things thro'
> narrow chinks of his cavern.

Blake was anticipating by more than a century the physics of relativity and quantum mechanics. Physicists, applying their "imaginative and immortal organs" to their visions from radio telescopes, electron microscopes and particle accelerators, have come to see scientifically that "Energy is the only life," and that our everyday perception of the universe as matter is a sort of hallucination operative only at a very gross and superficial level of perception. Solely by a counterintuitive process of "melting apparent surfaces away" can the scientist or the mystic discover "the infinite which was hid." In the psychopharmacology of the entheogens, we have the means to reconcile the unseen, mystical worlds of the physicists and poets. For the entheogens constitute, as Albert Hofmann asserted, something like "cracks in the infinite realm of matter," and operate "at the borderline where mind and matter merge" [Hofmann 1980,1989]. They are to philosophy and pharmacology what the radioactive isotopes are to physics—cracks in the materialistic edifice of reality, where matter spontaneously transforms, or profoundly alters consciousness.

Planet Earth, Our Lady Gæa, is suffering mightily the consequences of our materialistic world-view, especially the Judæo-Christian tendency to see humankind as a special creation, apart from all other Gæan life-forms, and as enjoined, moreover, to subdue and dominate other creatures. This horrendous duality is a modern superstition, for there is overwhelming scientific and experiential evidence which assures us that we are but one strand in the warp and weft of life; biochemically kindred to every other Gæan life-form and descended from the same primordial ancestors. This is a treacherous superstition, for placing of humankind above and

[88]

beyond Nature has led to the objectification of our planet and all her Gæan creatures. Instead of revering our planetary mother, from whose cavernous, salty womb we have miraculously leapt forth, we see only property... things to be bought and sold. Rather than marvel at the eternally ephemeral, living miracle that is each and every one of our feathered, furry, leafy, spiny or scaly brethren, we see only dinner, resources that can be exploited. And exploit them we do, so ruthlessly that the extinction of plant and animal species, nay, of entire habitats, is an everyday occurrence, and by the time it dawns on us that we, too, are on the endangered species list, it may be a trifle too late!

That is where *ayahuasca* comes into the picture, as a healing balm for the lesions of materialism... as a prospective *panacæa* for our great sweet mother *Pangæa*. For the essence of the entheogenic experience is ecstasy, in the original sense of the word *ek-stasis*—the "withdrawal of the soul from the body." It is an ineffable, spiritual, non-materialistic state of being in which the universe is experienced more as energy than as matter. It is Blake's Eternal Delight, the archetypal religious experience, the heart and soul of shamanism, the pinnacle of human achievement in the archaic, preliterate world. It is to see, as did Blake, that "every thing that lives is Holy," *us* included, and especially Our Lady Gæa, this living, breathing, growing and evolving biosphere... to realize that *every* place is a sacred place, for the universe itself is divine, it is our creator. We are Gæan creatures every one, woven of the clay of this watery blue planet (seasoned with a bit of star dust), but the Earthen atoms that continually flow and plait themselves through our bones and blood and sinew are animated into this ecstatic dance of life by thermonuclear stellar energy.

Shamanic ecstasy is the *real* "Old Time Religion," of which modern churches are but pallid evocations. Our forebears discovered in many times and places that in the ecstatic, entheogenic experience, suffering humankind could reconcile the cultivated braininess, which isolated each individual human being from all other creatures and even from other human beings, with the wild and feral, beastly magnificent bodies that we also are. Blake said it beautifully, that this Energy of life, this Eternal Delight is from the Body... this Body which might be seen as an elaborate energy-processing machine working to maintain consciousness in a biocomputer... or perchance the Body and the biocomputer alike are just elablorate mechanisms for perpetuating the replication of some invisible, diaphanous strands of nucleic acids! This *mysterium tremendum*, this *unio mystica*, this eternally delightful experience of the universe as energy, is a *sine qua non* of religion, *it is what religion is for!* There is no need for faith, it is the ecstatic experience itself that *gives* one faith in the intrinsic unity and integrity of the universe, in ourselves as integral parts of the whole; that reveals to us the sublime majesty of our universe, and the fluctuant, scintillant, alchemical miracle that is quotidian consciousness [Ott, in preparation].

We must come down from the Judæo-Christian pedestal and revel in our kinship with our fellow plant and animal creatures... we must repudiate religions which *defend against* religious experiences, wearily celebrating communion with a *placebo* sacrament, which requires faith and gives none! We must foster the Entheogenic Reformation, restoring the very heart and soul, yea, the core mystery to exsanguinated, purely theoretical religions which have lost touch with spirituality; hence all meaning and relevance. We must reject what Blake called "pale religious letchery" that heals not the gaping wound between Body and Soul, but would tear them asunder!

Entheogens like *ayahuasca* may be just the right medicine for hypermaterialistic humankind on the threshold of a new millennium which will determine whether our species continues to grow and prosper, or destroys itself in a massive biological Holocaust unlike anything the planet has experienced in the last 65 million years. Most of us really don't believe in the gods any more; few among us have much faith in our governments, nor in science and technology... but we *do* believe in the magic of drugs! We believe that shots can cure 'most anything... we don't want to be told that smoking, drinking alcohol, lack of exercise and poor diet may lead to coronary disease, we want a "magic bullet" that will make it go away instantly. We count on drugs to heal our ills, assuage our pain, to immobilize the violent, to wake us up, to put us to sleep, to make us sociable, to entertain us, to relax us, to make us smarter, to make us stronger athletes... drugs we believe in, O yes! It is a supreme irony that a material substance, a drug, could be the effective medicine against materialism:

> Perhaps with all our modern knowledge we do not need the divine mushrooms any more. Or do we need them more than ever? Some are shocked that the key even to religion might be reduced to a mere drug. On the other hand, the drug is as mysterious as it ever was: "like the wind it cometh we know not whence, nor why."

I venture to answer R. Gordon Wasson's rhetorical question: precisely *because of* our modern knowledge, *we need the divine entheogens more than ever.* Far from taking the mystery *out of* religion, the restoration of *genuine* entheogenic sacraments puts the Mystery *back into* religion, obviating the necessity of faith in sophistical doctrines. The Entheogenic Reformation is our best hope for healing Our Lady Gæa, while fostering a *genuine* religious revival for a new millennium. That revival is under way in the vast tent of this watery blue planet... Gi' me that Old Time Religion!

NOTES

[1] In 1978, R. Gordon Wasson convened an informal committee of researchers interested in the ethnopharmacognosy of shamanic inebriants, to look for a substitute for inadequate terms like "hallucinogenic" (which implied delusion and/or falsity, besides suggesting pathology to psychotherapists), "psychotomimetic" (implying also pathology) and "psychedelic" (besides being a pejorative term prejudicing shamanic inebriants in the eyes of persons unfamiliar with the field, this term had become so invested with connotations of 1960s western "counterculture" as to make it incongruous to speak of a shaman ingesting a *psychedelic* plant). I have summarized the history of *psychedelic* and *hallucinogenic* in my recent book *Pharmacotheon*. Members of our committee were classical scholars Carl A.P. Ruck and Danny Staples of Boston University, and independent ethnobotanists Jeremy Bigwood, Wasson and me. One of Ruck's early suggestions was *epoptic* from the Greek *epoptes* to describe initiates to the Eleusinian Mysteries who had seen *ta hiera*, "the holy." Wasson didn't like this term... as he said, it sounded like "pop, goes the weasel"! I proposed *pharmacotheon*, which had the advantage of already being in the *Oxford English Dictionary*, but it seemed too much of a mouthful, besides not adapting gracefully to the adjectival form. We finally settled on the neologism *entheogen[ic]*, from the Greek *entheos*, a term used by the ancient Greeks to describe prophetic or poetic inspiration. The term means literally "realizing the divine within," and can be seen as the user realizing that the divine infuses all of the creation, or specifically that the *entheogenic* plant is itself infused with the divine. It is *not* a theological term, makes no reference to any deity, and is not meant to be a pharmacological term for designating a specific chemical class of drugs (*psychedelic*, for example, has come to be seen by some *sensu strictu* as a term to designate mescaline-like β-phenethylamines or DMT-like tryptamines). Rather, it is a cultural term to include all the shamanic inebriants—sacraments, plant teachers, the stock-in-trade of shamans the world over. As Bernard Ortíz de Montellano has pointed out, this word best reflects traditional conceptions of shamanic inebriation, as indicated by ancient Náhuatl terms *itech quinehua* "it takes possession of him" or *itech quiza* "it comes out in him" to describe this [Ortíz de Montellano 1990]. We launched the neologism in the *Journal of Psychedelic Drugs*, in an issue which I edited and in which I suggested the name be changed to *Journal of Entheogenic Drugs* [Ruck *et al.* 1979]. This didn't come to pass, but I think it influenced the editors to change the name to *Journal of Psychoactive Drugs* two years

later, consigning *psychedelic* ever more to the obscurity it deserves. By my count, our new word has appeared in print in at least seven languages; the major European languages plus Catalan, and has been widely accepted by leading experts in the field. I expect the recent publication of my *Pharmacotheon* to establish the word solidly in the English-, German- and Spanish-speaking worlds.

2   Even with the limited availability of starting materials and chemical reagents under the modern "War on Drugs," LSD can be manufactured for a pittance. At the peak of its demand as the sixties gave way to the seventies, LSD sold for about U.S.$4000 *per* gram in the United States. A gram represents 10,000 doses of 100 mcg, or a wholesale cost of about $0.40 *per* dose. At this time, ergotamine tartrate, the most rational starting material for black-market manufacture of LSD, was selling for about $30,000 *per* kilogram, from which LSD could be made at about a 30% yield in primitive and large-scale conditions. Assuming 3 kg of ergotamine tartrate and $10,000 worth of ancillary reagents, equipment and collateral costs, one kilogram of LSD could be manufactured for roughly U.S.$100,000. This kilogram of LSD would represent 10 million doses, or a production cost of $0.01 *per* dose. Even when the wholesale value of LSD dropped below $2000 *per* gram in the late 1970s and early 1980s, this still represented 20-fold value added, a sizable profit margin. In the early days of the LSD market, doses of 250–300 mcg were sold, but the typical dose quickly dropped to 100 mcg, then below, and today more likely hovers around the 50 mcg level [Brown & Malone 1973; Marnell 1993; Ratcliffe 1973].

3   As I summarized in great detail in *Pharmacotheon*, there is much confusion in lay use of terminology relating to the provenience of drugs. The term *synthetic* refers to the manner of manufacture and is not a qualitative term. Drugs may be either *natural* (if they have been found to occur in plants or animals) or *artificial* (if they have not). Even *natural* drugs may be *synthetic*, if they are manufactured by human artifice. Psilocybine and DMT are examples of *synthetic natural products*, as these have mostly been laboratory-made. Any *artificial* drug can be assumed to be so only provisionally, as *artificial* compounds, crea- tions of the laboratory, frequently are found, with further research, to be *natural* drugs. Again, DMT is a perfect example. First synthesized in 1931, it existed as an *artificial* drug for 24 years, until it was definitively shown to be a *natural* drug and an active principle of *cohoba* or *yopo* snuff (see Chapter Two and *Pharmacotheon*) [Fish *et al.* 1955; Manske 1931; Ott 1993]. It is the height of folly and presumption to embrace some drugs, on the basis of their being *natural*, and to reject others, in the belief they are *artificial*— we can- not know which presumably *artificial* compounds will later, like DMT, *Valium* and poly- ester, be found in fact to be natural products!

4   In the ancient Indian *Ṛg Veda*, the oldest of the four *Vedas* and a fundamental sacred scrip- ture of Hinduism, which dates from the middle of the second millennium before the Christian era, exalted poetry is directed to *Soma* which was, at once, a god, a plant, and the juice of that plant. R. Gordon Wasson devoted the better part of a decade to concerted study of *Soma*, and his book *Soma: Divine Mushroom of Immortality*, besides being a masterpiece of the writer's and bookmaker's art, is one of the greatest and most important

scientific books of all history [Wasson 1968]. The *Rg Veda* repeatedly refers to the *Soma* potion—most decidedly an entheogen, as Vedist Wendy Doniger has asserted—by the name *amrta* (sometimes written *amrita* or *amreeta*, as it would be pronounced) [Doniger O'Flaherty 1982]. This word would be translated as "pharmacotheon" or "entheogen," 'though the *Oxford English Dictionary* gives "immortal, ambrosial." Indeed, the cognate term in Greek is *ambrosia*, the legendary food or, more precisely, drink of the Olympian gods, which was obviously in origin an entheogen like *Soma*, if not identical to it (indeed, the evidence would indicate that both *Soma/amrta* and *ambrosia/nectar* were originally entheogenic mushrooms). The interested reader is referred to my yet-unfinished *Pharmacotheon II: Entheogenic Plants and the Origins of Religions* [Ott, in preparation].

5   From the time of the *Rg Veda*, *circa* 1500 B.C. to the end of the fourth century of our era, there was celebrated an annual initiation into the sacred Mysteries of Eleusis at a temple near Athens. Anyone speaking Greek and having the price of admission was accepted for initiation, but only once in a lifetime. Most of the leading intellectuals of antiquity were initiates, and many testified to the value of the experience which was "new, astonishing, inaccessible to rational cognition." Of the experience initiates or *mystes* could only say they had see *ta hiera*, "the holy"——it was forbidden by law, under penalty of death, to say more. From the fragmentary hints of several writers, from an anonymous eighth century B.C. poem called the *Homeric Hymn to Demeter* (which described the founding of the Mystery by Demeter, grief-stricken over the abduction of her daughter Persephone by Hades), from a fresco at Pompeii, we know that the initiates drank a potion called the *kykeon* or "mixture" preparatory to experiencing a soul-shattering vision which was forever to enrich their lives and convert them into *epoptes*, those who had seen. In 1978 R. Gordon Wasson, Albert Hofmann and Carl A.P. Ruck unveiled the hoary secret of the Mysteries which had been guarded for 3500 years, when they proposed that the *kykeon* was an entheogenic potion containing LSD-like ergoline alkaloids. The reader is referred to their book *The Road to Eleusis: Unveiling the Secret of the Mysteries* [Wasson *et al.* 1978] for details, and to my *Pharmacotheon* [Ott 1993] for a summary of this theory.

6   The name of the ancient classical Mother Earth Goddess is spelled either Gaia or Gæa. The former is pronounced as in German *Gäa*, "**gay** uh," although the strange mispronunciation "**guy** uh" has taken root in the English-speaking world, making the name of the most feminine of deities sound almost masculine! The alternate orthography, Gæa, is pronounced "**jee** uh" (as in *Pangæa*, the primordial super-continent of geological [Gæa-logical] plate-tectonics theory). Since I have subtitled this book *Pangæan Entheogens* to highlight the cosmopolitan nature of *ayahuasca* analogues, I have decided to spell her name Gæa (*Gea* in Spanish). An obsolete name for the Old World is *Palæogæa*. I refer to the "evil and hypocritical, fifteen-hundred-and-ninety-eight-year-old crusade to eliminate this class of drugs from the face of the Earth," dating from the destruction of the Eleusinian sanctuary by Alaric's Goths in 396 A.D. This event marked the demise of organized pagan religion in the Mediterranean basin, and the decisive downfall of the classical world.

7   Authors of the earliest treatises on entheogenic drugs, dating from the middle of the last

century, chose to call these substances "narcotics." Ernst Freiherrn von Bibra's seminal *Die Narkotischen Genußmittel und der Mensch* (*Narcotic Dainties and Humankind*) [1855], James F. Johnston's *The Chemistry of Common Life*, with eight chapters on "The Narcotics we Indulge In" [1853-1855] and Mordecai Cubitt Cooke's *The Seven Sisters of Sleep. Popular History of the Seven Prevailing Narcotics of the World* [1860] all made this association. When Richard Spruce first reported his studies of *ayahuasca* and entheogenic snuffs, he called them "remarkable narcotics" [1873]. The word *narcotic*, however, derives from the Greek word ναρκωτικ–υμ, "to benumb, to stupefy," supporting the definition of *narcotic* as: "inducing stupor, sleep, or insensibility" [*Oxford English Dictionary*, Compact Edition, p. 1895]. This is precisely the opposite of the effect of entheogens, which are potent stimulants, antagonists to sleep, and sensitizing agents! I have summarized the modern misuse of *narcotic* in this context in *Pharmacotheon*, commenting also that the word is decidedly pejorative in that it has acquired a modern sense of "an illicit substance." Anyone sensitive to the nuances and politics of language would be loathe to associate the term *narcotic* with the entheogens [Ott 1993].

[8] Chemical analyses of a botanically-undocumented entheogenic *epená* snuff prepared by Venezuelan Surará Indians found harmine and *d*-leptaflorine, plus traces of harmaline in the powder [Bernauer 1964; Holmstedt & Lindgren 1967]. Although various β-carboline alkaloids are indeed known from *Virola* species used in these snuffs, these three have never been found in *Virola* and are definite signatures of *Banisteriopsis* and other Malpighiaceae used in *ayahuasca*. These same three β-carbolines were also isolated from the stem of a liana—evidently *Banisteriopsis*— said to have been used in preparation of *paricá* snuff by Tukano and Tariana Indians of the Río Negro [Biocca *et al.* 1964]. There is thus some evidence for the involvement of *Banisteriopsis* in the South American snuff complex, and Holmstedt & Lindgren [1967] commented on the possibility of an *ayahuasca*-type pharmacological synergy between β-carbolines and tryptamines in the snuffs (see page 49).

[9] The murals in the great Meso-American metropolis of Teotihuacan are eloquent graphic pæans to the sacred entheogens. Disembodied eyes abound, which Wasson has proposed to be a simple and natural glyph representative of the visionary eye of the seer inebriated with entheogenic plants [Wasson 1980]. The lovely murals are found in numerous low, labyrinthine buildings which evidently served as *cenacula* for the sacramental ingestion of wondrous mushrooms, *ololiuhqui*, *Ska Pastora* and the other Mexican entheogens (see my *Pharmacotheon* for details on Mexican shamanic inebriants; Ott 1993). The murals depict roving disembodied eyes, and entheogenic plants whose flowers are "all eyes" and from which flowers exude droplets of entheogenic potion with appended disembodied eyes. Indeed, what could these "disembodied eye drops" represent, other than the entheogenic visionary potion issuing from entheogenic flowers [Ott & Wasson 1983]? To the ancient Aztecs, "flowers" (*xóchitl* or *ihuinti*) was a metaphor for entheogenic plants, and even flowerless mushrooms were called *xochinanácatl*—"flower mushrooms," entheogenic mushrooms. When the murals show "speech scrolls" adorned with flowers, this must represent the *logos* or oracular speech of the priest immersed in a *temicxoch* or "flowery dream"—entheogenic dream—as expressed in *tecpillatolli*, the sacred language of priests

and of poets [Cáceres 1984; León Portilla 1961; Ortíz de Montellano 1990; Ott 1993].

[10] During the 1977 Alpha Helix Amazon Expedition, extracts were made of fresh material of *Brunfelsia grandiflora* subsp. *schultesii* bark, which "contained large quantities of sco-poletine which was shown to process [*sic*] psychopharmacological activity in mice." However, the scopoletine-free fraction was further fractionated, and appeared also to be active. The pharmacology of these intriguing plants remains to be completely resolved [Schultes & Hofmann 1980].

[11] Besides the problem of the analysis of a sample of *ayahuasca* which had been kept more than two years without refrigeration, the 1970 paper by the Der Marderosian group is difficult to interpret owing to some apparent typographical errors. Although the potion reportedly contained 0.007% harmine and 0.011% harmaline, the authors claimed to have effected "the separation of crystalline DMT and harmine from it." Had harmaline in fact been present at a concentration 50% greater than harmine, it seems most unlikely that the less-concentrated of these two alkaloids (which are very similar chemically) would have crystallized out. In their conclusions the authors vaguely stated the typical dose contained "about 0.02 g of harmine or harmaline," noting that "frequently two or three times this dose is consumed" [Der Marderosian *et al.* 1970]. Given the other evidence showing harmine and *d*-leptaflorine to be the major alkaloids of *ayahuasca*, with harmaline as a trace constituent, and these authors' report of having crystallized *harmine*, not harmaline from the potion, the report of 50% more harmaline than harmine seems anomalous. The failure to report detection of *d*-leptaflorine is another anomaly.

[12] Besides *Banisteriopsis caapi* samples from the Culina and Sharanahua Indians, Rivier and Lindgren [1972] analyzed samples from mestizo *ayahuasqueros* of Iquitos and Tarapoto, Perú, finding 0.57% and 0.83% alkaloids respectively, with leaves of *cielo ayahuasca* from Iquitos containing 0.25%. McKenna later reported a *cielo ayahuasca* sample from Iquitos to contain 0.17% alkaloids [McKenna *et al.* 1984a]. Rivier and Lindgren also analyzed a mestizo sample from Río Ucayali, and samples from Ecuador and Brazil, as well as from Piro Indians of Perú and Marinahua Indians of the upper Río Purús area.

[13] McKenna's [1984a] group also analyzed freeze-dried *ayahuasca* samples from Iquitos and Tarapoto, Perú, but provided no information on preparation or dosage levels. The sole sample from Tarapoto contained 0.29% total alkaloids (50% harmine, 36% *d*-leptaflorine, 14% harmaline and no DMT). This sample had been prepared with *Psychotria carthagenensis* [*sic*], analysis of which had failed to detect DMT. Three different samples of Iquitos *ayahuasca* contained 0.67, 0.31 and 0.32% alkaloids (average 0.43%), of which 42, 33 and 27% (average 34%) was harmine; 38, 33 and 30% (average 34%) *d*-leptaflorine; 9, 17, 20% (average 15%) harmaline and 11, 8, 2% (average 7%) DMT. Assuming a dose of 100 ml, these would average out to 397 mg total alkaloids, with 135 mg each of harmine and *d*-leptaflorine, 60 mg harmaline and 28 mg DMT.

[14] Even an old sample of crystalline harmaline from a large German chemical/pharmaceutical

company was found on analysis to consist of a mixture of roughly two parts harmaline to one part harmine, the latter evidently a decomposition product [Shulgin 1993].

[15] Turner and Merlis conducted experiments on 14 "schizophrenics" in a New York mental institution, whom they treated like so many guinea pigs. They began conducting tests with bufotenine, a noxious, non-entheogenic tryptamine (5-hydroxy-DMT) which had already been shown by Howard D. Fabing and J. Robert Hawkins [1956] to provoke life-threatening circulatory crises, turning the faces of four unfortunate Ohio State Peniten-tiary inmates "the color of an eggplant" diluted! Turner and Merlis also found dramatic circulatory crises following intravenous administration of 10 mg bufotenine to one of their helpless "patients," and only ceased abusing bufotenine when three of their "pa-tients" nearly died after relatively small doses of the drug. Unbelievably, Turner and Merlis injected their charges with the dangerous drug "as they were coming out of insulin coma or following EST" (electroshock so-called "therapy"), as well as after pretreatment with chlorpromazine and reserpine. In the two cases involving reserpine and chlorpromazine, "each of these [bufotenine] injections almost proved fatal in small amounts (between 2.5 and 5.0 mg)" with cessation of breathing and the characteristic cyanosis, cavalierly described as a "plum-colored" face! The "patients became frightened to an extreme degree," which indicates they weren't too far out of touch to perceive that their physicians (and jailers) were trying to kill them! Just getting warmed up, the Drs. Hyde proceeded to experiments involving intramuscular injections of DMT into ten "patients." Although 5–20 mg DMT intranasally and up to 350 mg orally were inactive, 25 mg intramuscular injections of the drug were impressively active, with "one or more evidences of fear" in each of the nine subjects receiving this dose. One "patient" reportedly said after a 25 mg injection of DMT, "You frighten me. What have you done to me?" Nevertheless, the mad doctors responded *by increasing the dose* to 50 mg in subsequent tests. Only when a female "patient" almost died from cardiac arrest after a 40 mg injection ("extreme cyanosis quick-ly developed"), being without pulse for 30 seconds and necessitating cardiac massage to save her, were the good doctors scared into a semblance of caution. Fifteen minutes after her near-fatal injection of DMT, the wretched woman was "able to see well, and to respond to a microphone by saying: 'Take that away. I don't like them.'" Even 'though Turner and Merlis treated these ill-starred "patients" like so many laboratory animals, by their recorded responses they sound quite rational and aware of what was happening to them. Naturally, Turner and Merlis did not try these murderous experiments on themselves, their only psychonautic foray was with a Peruvian *yopo* snuff obtained from Siri von Reis, with which "one of us first endeavored [unsuccessfully] to produce an intoxication in himself. Thereafter, schizophrenic subjects were tested throughout." I call this experiment unethical and cite it as an example of drug abuse, because the only ethical way to test prospective psychoactive drugs is on oneself, in self-experiments, to establish basic parameters of toxicity and dosage (see Note 18). Only when the safety of a preparation has been thereby established, could it be ethical to conduct further tests in fully-informed volunteers. The Nürnberg War Crimes Tribunal sentenced some German physicians, who had experimented on concentration-camp prisoners at Dachau and elsewhere, to the gallows for experiments similar to those conducted by Fabing and Hawkins at the Ohio

State Penitentiary, and by Turner and Merlis at the New York mental "hospital." The tribunals led to a code of ethics governing all medical experimentation, mandating full voluntary consent on the part of human subjects of any medical experiments [Annas & Grodin 1992]. No prisoner nor mental patient can be said to consent freely to such experiments, their confinement and destitute condition precluding the possibility of their deciding objectively and freely. The U.S. government, meanwhile, under the ægis of the CIA project MKULTRA, was experimenting with some 800 drugs, including bufotenine, on prisoners at the U.S. Public Health Service Addiction Research Center Hospital [*sic*] in Lexington, Kentucky. In this publicly-funded institution, existing ostensibly to "cure" drug addiction, Harris S. Isbell obtained "voluntary consent" from his "patients" (since the institution was officially categorized as a penitentiary, perhaps they might better be called "prisoners") by offering payment in kind—injections of heroin and morphine were administered as payment for cooperation in the experiments [Lee & Shlain 1985; Marks 1979]! These are all classic examples of how to abuse entheogenic drugs—giving them to unwilling (or unwitting) subjects—and are all textbook examples of unethical experimentation. Ethical procedures for human testing of novel psychoactive agents have been admirably established and followed by the group of Alexander T. Shulgin, whose human testing of some 179 novel psychotropic agents is described in his recent book with wife Ann Shulgin, *PIHKAL: A Chemical Love Story* [Shulgin & Shulgin 1991].

[16] There has been a lamentable confusion in the scientific literature between harmine, the main alkaloid of *ayahuasca*, and harmaline, which has received much more attention. As I explained in a detailed footnote in *Pharmacotheon*, at least six publications have confused harmine and harmaline, especially Peter Stafford's *Psychedelics Encyclopedia* [Stafford 1983]. One of the papers most responsible for this confusion was Claudio Naranjo's 1973 paper (based on experiments already described from an earlier paper) "Psychological Aspects of the *Yagé* [*sic*]Experience in an Experimental Setting" [Naranjo 1967,1973]. This paper was mistitled, as it did not involve experimental tests of *yajé* at all, but rather detailed previously-published human studies of β-carbolines, chiefly harmaline. Not only is harmaline a trace constituent in *ayahuasca* beverages studied, and appears to play little or no role in *ayahuasca* pharmacology but, as we will see, it is the DMT which accounts for the entheogenic properties of *ayahuasca*, not the β-carbolines. Naranjo's paper in reality had nothing to do with the the pharmacology of *ayahuasca*, and should have been titled "Psychological Aspects of the *Harmaline* Experience in an Experimental Setting." The reader is referred to *Pharmacotheon*, Chapter 3, Note 3, for a study of the incredible confusion spawned by Naranjo's error [Ott 1993].

[17] Although Hochstein and Paradies [1957] were the first chemists to associate DMT with *ayahuasca*, which later proved to be an important and key discovery, not only did they fail to deposit "voucher specimens" of the source plant (these are dried and pressed botanical specimens, suitable for later botanical identification, deposited in a recognized herbarium, enabling scientists later to "vouch" for the identification), they in fact never even saw it. In their paper, these American drug company (Pfizer, Inc.) chemists stated: "A second plant, 'Yage,' *Prestonia amazonicum* (*Haemadictyon amazonicum* Spruce) was

made available to us as an aqueous extract of the leaves." They were able to isolate a substantial quantity of DMT, purified as the free base, from this extract. The extract was collected by a D.H. Allen on the Río Napo near Iquitos, Perú, and supposedly represented an infusion of leaves used in *ayahuasca*, "in the belief that the... [leaf admixture] suppresses the more unpleasant hallucinations associated with pure *B. caapi* extracts." Supposedly a Dr. R. Ferreyra of the Universidad de San Marcos in Lima, Perú made the botanical determination. Although, as I pointed out in Chapter One, the name *Prestonia amazonica* has long been associated with *ayahuasca*, this plant has never been documented to be used in the potions and Schultes was later told by Ferreyra that no botanical specimens existed to support this identification (this botanist had evidently suggested to Hochstein and Paradies, based on the [erroneous] literature, that *P. amazonica* was a possible identification for the *ayahuasca* leaf admixture) [Schultes & Raffauf 1960]. DMT, moreover, is not known from authentic material of this species, nor from any other species of Apocynaceae. Although Bristol [1966] suggested that *Banisteriopsis rusbyana* (=*Diplopterys cabrerana*) might have been the source of the leaf extract, a more probable source was *Psychotria viridis* or a related *Psychotria* species, which are much more commonly used as *ayahuasca* admixtures in Perú, particularly in the Iquitos area, than is *Diplopterys cabrerana* [McKenna *et al.* 1984a].

[18] I employ the term "Heffter Technique" in honor of German chemist Arthur Heffter from Leipzig, who isolated four pure alkaloids from dried *péyotl*, *Lophophora williamsii*, in the mid-1890s. Since animal experiments were worthless to sort out the entheogenic effect from other pharmacological noise, Heffter tested his alkaloids on himself, in an heroic series of self-experiments culminating on 23 November 1897, when he ingested 150 mg of *Mezcalin* (today spelled mescalin[e]) hydrochloride which he correctly identified as the entheogenic principle of the drug [Heffter 1896, 1898]. This was the world's first trip with a purified chemical compound. A self-experimenter like Heffter was later aptly characterized by famed German writer Ernst Jünger, in his logbook of personal drug experimentation, *Annäherungen: Drogen und Rausch (Approximations: Drugs and Inebriation)*, as a *psychonaut*, a voyager employing entheogenic drugs as his vehicle [Jünger 1970]. There has long been scientific controversy regarding the validity of self-experiments by scientists, who supposedly thereby sacrificed their "scientific objectivity" (whatever that is). As R. Gordon Wasson, himself accused of such loss of scientific objectivity for his psychonautic expeditions with mushrooms and psilocybine, commented: "Thus it comes about that we are all divided into two classes: those who have taken the mushroom and are disqualified by our subjective experience, and those who have not taken the mushroom and are disqualified by their total ignorance of the subject!" [Wasson 1961]. It should be noted that not only mescaline, but the two other primary entheogens LSD and psilocybine, were all discovered by psychonauts, chemists evaluating their chemical fractions in self-experiments. Chemists, like Louis Lewin, who attempted to isolate the entheogenic principle of *péyotl*, and like James Moore, who tried to isolate the active principles of *teonanácatl* mushrooms, by relying exclusively on animal assays, uniformly failed. Similarly, on the basis of animal tests in 1938, pharmacologists at Sandoz Ltd. had determined that Albert Hofmann's LSD was of little pharmacological interest. It was only

because Hofmann had a "striking presentiment" that LSD possessed activity which the pharmacologists had missed, that he decided to prepare a second batch of the drug five years later. This hunch, combined with his serendipitous discovery of its effects in himself, quite by accident, led him to conduct a bioassay with the "intact Albert Hofmann preparation" three days later, leading to the discovery that LSD was the most powerful enarheogenic agent known [Hofmann 1980; Ott 1993]. Not only is self-experimentation by scientists a valid procedure on scientific grounds, it likely is the *only* bioassay that works—the effect being sought may be specific to the human nervous system. Scientists have wasted much time and effort in vain pursuit of an elusive animal model of "hallucinosis," having used spiders, cats, simians, even elephants [Cohen 1964; Díaz 1975]. Not only is the Heffter Technique the best and possibly only valid bioassay for entheogenic effects, it is, as we saw in Note 15, *the only ethical way to conduct this sort of research.* Of course, those opposed to use of animals as research subjects would agree, on ethical grounds. There are thus compelling practical, scientific and ethical reasons for my choice of the "intact Jonathan Ott preparation" as bioassay to resolve *ayahuasca* pharmacology.

[19] I have chosen to call my psychonautic experiments "travels in the universe of the soul" after the title of a moving and important paper by Rudolf Gelpke, "Von Fahrten in den Weltraum der Seele: Berichte über Selbstversuche mit Delysid (LSD) und Psilocybin (CY)," a pioneering and beautifully-written account of 6 of 19 psychonautic experiments with pharmaceutical *Delysid*® (LSD) and *Indocybin*® (psilocybine), originally published in *Antaios* under the editorship of Ernst Jünger and Mircea Eliade [Gelpke 1962]. Since I felt these were some of the most poetic descriptions of entheogenic voyages yet penned, I laboriously translated the paper into English and published it in *Journal of Psychoactive Drugs* under the same title, "Travels in the Universe of the Soul: Reports on Self-Experiments with Delysid (LSD) and Psilocybin (CY)" [Gelpke 1981]. I commend also to my readers' attention Dr. Gelpke's superb book *Vom Rausch im Orient und Okzident* (*On Inebriation in the Orient and Occident*; also published under the title *Drogen und Seelenerweiterung* or *Drugs and Mind-Expansion*) [Gelpke 1966]. This Islamic scholar tragically died in 1972, aged 44. Gelpke was a friend of Albert Hofmann and Ernst Jünger, and Jünger described LSD and psilocybine experiments he conducted together with Rudolf Gelpke and others in his excellent book *Annäherungen* (see previous note) [Jünger 1970].

[20] As I outlined in my recent book *Pharmacotheon* [Ott 1993], the current legal status of religions employing illegal entheogens as sacraments is confused by legal contradictions and ambivalent judicial decisions. Whereas 23 states specifically exempt members of the *péyotl*-using Native American Church from controlled substances laws (*péyotl* and its main active principle, mescaline, are Schedule I drugs), and whereas the "American Indian Religious Freedom Act" [42 USC 1996, P.L. 95–341] of 1978 allegedly protects American Indians' religious freedom, there have been sporadic arrests of Indian peyotlists. The State of Texas adopted a law requiring at least 25% Indian blood as a prerequisite for Church membership, and the national directorate (but not all local chapters) also adopted this racist standard. A 1979 federal court ruling in New York [Native American Church *v.* U.S.D.C.N.Y., 1979, 468 F. Suppl. 1247, affirmed 633 F. 2d 205] held that "the use of

peyote for sacramental purposes... is not to be restricted to the Native American Church." The same year, the all-race "The Peyote Way Church of God" was chartered in Arizona (where *péyotl* doesn't grow), and the following year Church members were arrested in Texas (the only U.S. state where *péyotl* grows naturally) for possession of the sacrament! Charges were subsequently dropped, and the Church filed a discrimination complaint against the State of Texas. What is sorely needed is a uniform ruling from the U.S. Supreme Court, which dodged the issue in a recent case [Employment Division, Department of Human Resources of the State of Oregon, et al. *v.* Alfred L. Smith et al.; No. 86–946] involving the firing of Indian peyotlists (ironically, from state jobs as drug counselors) and subsequent denial of state benefits. The U.S. Supreme Court first remanded the case to the Oregon Supreme Court for a ruling as to legality of sacramental *péyotl* use in Oregon, essentially upholding states' rights with regard to religious exercise. The Oregon court, which had found against the State, conceded that Oregon had no legal exemption for sacramental *péyotl* use. The U.S. Supreme Court then reversed by a 6–3 vote, holding that there was a difference between religious beliefs and practices, and that an anti-drug law not intended to restrict religion was constitutional, even if it had that indirect result! Justice Scalia wrote the majority opinion, and Justice O'Connor concurred but argued over technicalities. The court ruling basically stated that "compelling" state security interests (in this case, the "necessity" of illegalizing "dangerous drugs") took precedence over details of religious practice (in this case, the use of a *real*, as opposed to a *placebo*, sacrament!). In a strong dissent, Justice Blackmun (joined by Justices Brennan and Marshall), alleged that "hysteria" over drugs had unduly influenced the Court to overturn a tradition of protection of religious practice. Blackmun also pointed out that, inasmuch as there is virtually no unlawful commerce in *péyotl*, and the goals and ideals of the Native American Church were not incompatible with values promoted by the State, that there was no state security interest to take precedence over religious freedom. Instead of taking this opportunity to clarify and standardize federal and state law with regard to religious sacraments that happen to be illegal drugs, the Supreme Court chose instead obfuscation and legal sophistry, in the process eroding still further our constitutional rights. How could the Supreme Court hear this case and not so much as mention the 1979 New York federal court ruling, which still stands as a precedent, and opens the door to the sincere, sacramental use of *péyotl* and other entheogens by anyone in the United States?

[21] Hordenine, or peyocactin, is a stimulant found in whole *Desmodium gangeticum* at a level of 0.05% and in *Dutaillyea oreophila* leaves at 0.013% [Baudouin *et al.* 1981]. In addition to tryptamines, branches and leaves of *Melicope leptococca* contained acronydine, kokusaginine, acronycidine, melicopicine, melicopidine, acronycine, 6-methoxy-2-methyl-tetrahydro-β-carboline and 3-dimethylaminoacetyl-5-methoxyindole. While 5-MeO-DMT was the principal alkaloid (35% of alkaloid fraction), it was followed closely by kokusaginine (30% of total alkaloids, or 0.18%). Kokusaginine is of unknown toxicity, and also occurs in leaves of *Dutaillyea oreophila* and stem bark of *D. drupacea* [Baudouin *et al.* 1981]. Kokusaginine occurs in leaves of *Vepris ampody* together with evoxanthine, phenylacetamide, 2,4-dimethoxy-10-methyl-acridanone and three novel quinolone alkaloids. In this case, DMT represented 80% of the alkaloid fraction [Kan-Fan *et al.* 1970].

Bibliography

Abu Zarga, M.H. 1986. "Three new simple indole alkaloids from *Limonia acidissima*" *Journal of Natural Products* 49(5): 901–904.

Agurell, S. *et al.* 1968. "Alkaloid content of *Banisteriopsis rusbyana*" *American Journal of Pharmacy* 140(5): 148–151.

Agurell, S. *et al.* 1969. "Alkaloids in certain species of *Virola* and other South American plants of ethnopharmacologic interest" *Acta Chemica Scandinavica* 23(3): 903–916.

Alarcón, R. 1990. Personal communications, Jatun Sacha, Ecuador.

Albarracín, L. 1925. *Contribución al Estudio de los Alcaloides de Yagé.* Thesis, Universidad Nacional, Bogotá, Colombia.

Allen, J.R.F. and **B.R. Holmstedt** 1980. "The simple β-carboline alkaloids" *Phytochemistry* 19: 1573–1582.

Anderson, E.F. 1980. *Peyote: The Divine Cactus.* Univ. of Arizona Press, Tucson, AZ.

Andritsky, W. 1988. *Schamanismus und Rituelles Heilen im Alten Peru.* Two volumes, Berlin, Germany.

Annas, G.J. and **M.A. Grodin** [Eds.] 1992. *The Nazi Doctors and the Nuremberg Code.* Oxford University Press, New York.

Anon. 1855. "Journal of a voyage up the Amazon and Río Negro by Richard Spruce, San Carlos del Río Negro, June 27, 1853" *Hooker Journal of Botany and Kew Garden Miscellany* Numbers 6 & 7.

Arévalo Valera, G. 1986. "El *ayahuasca* y el curandero Shipibo-Conibo del Ucayali (Perú)" *América Indígena* 46(1): 147–161.

Arispe, V.V. 1938. *Estudio Farmacográfico y Farmacológico del Ayahuasca.* Thesis, Universidad Nacional Mayor, Lima, Perú.

Arnold, O.H. and **G. Hofmann** 1957. "Zur Psychopathologie des Dimethyl-tryptamin" *Wiener Zeitschrift für Nervenheilkunde* 13: 438–445.

Arthur, H.R. *et al.* 1967. "N_b-Methylated tryptamines and other constituents of *Acacia confusa* Merr. of Hong Kong" *Australian Journal of Chemistry* 20: 811–813.

Baer, G. 1969. "Eine Ayahuasca-Sitzung unter den Piro (Ost-Perú)" *Bulletin de la Société Suisse des Américanistes* 33: 5–8.

Baer, G. and **W.W. Snell** 1974. "An ayahuasca ceremony among the Matsigenka (Eastern Peru)" *Zeitschrift für Ethnologie* 99(1&2): 64–80.

Balsam, G. and **H.W. Voigtländer** 1978. "Ein psychotropes Alkaloid aus Pilocarpus organensis" *Archiv der Pharmazie* 311: 1016–1018.

Banerjee, P.K. and **S. Ghosal** 1969. "Simple indole bases of *Desmodium gangeticum* (Leguminosae)" *Australian Journal of Chemistry* 22: 275–277.

Barnes, R.F. *et al.* 1971. "Evaluation of selected clones of *Phalaris arundinacea* II. Indole alkaloid derivatives" *Agronomy Journal* 63: 507–509.

Barriga Villalba, A.M. 1925a. "Un nuevo alcaloide" *Boletín de la Sociedad Colombiana de Ciencias Naturales* 14(79): 31–36.

Barriga Villalba, A.M. 1925b. "Yagéin: Ein neues Alkaloid" *Journal of the Society of Chemistry and Industry* 44: 205–207.

Baudouin, G. *et al.* 1981. "Plantes de Nouvelle-Calédonie. LXXIII. Alcaloïdes de *Dutaillyea oreophila* et de *Dutaillyea drupacea*" *Journal of Natural Products* 44(5): 546–550.

Baxter, C. and M. Slaytor 1972. "Biosynthesis and turnover of *N,N*-dimethyltryptamine and 5-methoxy-*N,N*-dimethyltryptamine in *Phalaris tuberosa*" *Phytochemistry* 11: 2767–2773.

Beer, A.G. 1939a. "Beiträge zur Pharmakologie des extrapyramidalen Systems. I. Mitteilung: Die Wirkung des Harmins bei Katzen mit intaktem Nervensystem" *Naunyn Schmiedeberg's Archiv für Experimentelle Pathologie und Pharmakologie* 193: 377–392.

Beer, A.G. 1939b. "Beiträge zur Pharmakologie des extrapyramidalen Systems. II. Mitteilung: Die Wirkung des Harmins bei Katzen ohne Neocortex" *Naunyn Schmiedeberg's Archiv für Experimentelle Pathologie und Pharmakologie* 193: 393–407.

Bellier, I. 1986. "Los cantos Mai Huna del yajé (Amazonia peruana)" *América Indígena* 46(1): 129–145.

Beringer, K. 1927. *Der Meskalinrausch: Seine Geschichte und Erscheinungsweise.* Springer-Verlag, Berlin, Germany. Reprint 1969.

Beringer, K. 1928. "Über ein neues, auf das extra-pyramidal-motorische System wirkendes Alkaloid (Banisterin)" *Der Nervenärzt* 1: 265–275.

Beringer, K. 1929. "Zur Banisterin- und Harminfrage" *Der Nervenärzt* 2: 548–549.

Beringer, K. and K. Wilmanns 1929. "Zur Harmin-Banisterin-Frage" *Deutscher Medizinischer Wochenschrift* 55: 2081–2086.

Bernauer, K. 1964. "Notiz über die Isolierung von Harmin und (+)-1,2,3,4-Tetrahydro-harmin aus einer indianischen Schnupfdroge" *Helvetica Chimica Acta* 47(4): 1075–1077.

Bhattacharya, S.K. *et al.* 1971. "Investigations on the hallucinogenic activity of indole alkylamines isolated from *Mucuna pruriens* DC" *Indian Journal of Physiology* 25(2): 53–56.

Bibra, E.F. von 1855. *Die Narkotischen Genußmittel und der Mensch.* Verlag von Wilhelm Schmid, Nürnberg, Germany.

Bigwood, J.E. 1978. Personal communications, Shelton, WA.

Bigwood, J.E. and J. Ott 1977. "DMT" *Head.* November issue. pp. 56 *et seq.*

Biocca, E.F. *et al.* 1964. "Sulla sostanze allucinogene impiegata in Amazonia. Nota I. Osservazioni sul paricá dei Tukâno e Tariâna del bacino del Río Uaupés" *Annali di Chimica* 54: 1175–1178.

Bisset, N.G. 1992. "War and hunting poisons of the New World. Part 1. Notes on the early history of curare" *Journal of Ethnopharmacology* 36(1): 1–26.

Blake, W. [A. Kazin, Ed.] 1946. *The Portable Blake.* The Viking Press, New York.

Bohinc, P. *et al.* 1977. "Xanthine alkaloids in *Ilex ambigua* leaves" *Farmacevtski Vestnik* 28: 89–96.

Boom, B.M. and S. Moestl 1990. "Ethnobotanical notes of José M. Cruxent from the Franco-Venezuelan expedition to the headwaters of the Orinoco River, 1951–1952" *Economic Botany* 44(3): 416–419.

Böszörményi, Z. and G. Brunecker 1957. "Dimethyltryptamine (DMT) experiments with psychotics" In: Garattini, S. and V. Ghetti [Eds.] *Psychotropic Drugs.* Elsevier, Amsterdam, Netherlands. pp. 580–581.

Böszörményi, Z. and S.I. Szára 1958. "Dimethyltryptamine experiments with psychotics" *Journal of Mental Science* 104: 445–453.

Bristol, M.L. 1966. "The psychotropic *Banisteriopsis* among the Sibundoy of Colombia"

Botanical Museum Leaflets Harvard University 21(5): 113–140.

Bristol, M.L. *et al.* 1969. "The alkaloids of the genus *Datura*, section *Brugmansia*. Part VI. Tree *Datura* drugs (*Datura candida* cvs) of the Colombian Sibundoy" *Lloydia* 32: 123–130.

Brown, J.K. and M.H. Malone [Eds.] 1973. "Status of drug quality in the street-drug market" *Pacific Information Service on Street-Drugs* 3(1): 1–7.

Brückl, K. and F. Mussgnug 1929. "Über die Identität von Harmin und Banisterin" *Münchner Medizinischer Wochenschrift* 26: 1078.

Brunner, H.G. *et al.* 1993. "Abnormal behavior associated with a point mutation in the structural gene for monoamine oxidase A" *Science* 262: 578–580.

Brüzzi A. da S., A. 1962. *A Civilização Indigena do Uaupés*. Linográfica, São Paolo, Brasil.

Buckholtz, N.S. and W.O. Boggan 1977. "Monoamine oxidase inhibition in brain and liver produced by β-carbolines: Structure-activity relationships and substrate specificity" *Biochemical Pharmacology* 26: 1991–1996.

Burroughs, W.S. and A. Ginsberg 1963. *The Yage Letters*. City Lights, San Francisco, CA.

Cáceres, A. 1984. *In Xóchitl in Cuicatl: Hallucinogens and Music in Mesoamerican Amerindian Thought*. Thesis, University of Indiana, Bloomington, IN.

Calella, P. de 1935. "Los indios Sionas del Putumayo" *Boletín de Estudios Históricos* 73-74: 49–52.

Calella, P. de 1944a. "Datos mitológicos de los Huitotos de La Chorrera" *Amazonia Colombiana Americanista* 2(4-8): 33–37.

Calella, P. de 1944b. "Breves notas mitológicas de los Huitotos de Santa Clara" *Amazonia Colombiana Americanista* 2(4-8): 38–40.

Callaway, J.C. 1988. "A proposed mechanism for the visions of dream sleep" *Medical Hypotheses* 26: 119–124.

Callaway, J.C. 1992. Personal communications, San Luis Potosí, México.

Callaway, J.C. 1993. "Tryptamines, β-carbolines and you" *MAPS* 4(2): 30–32.

Calvo, C. 1981. *Las Tres Mitades de Ino Moxo y Otros Brujos [sic] de la Amazonia*. Proceso Editores, Iquitos, Perú.

Carneiro, R.L. 1980. "Chimera of the Upper Amazon" In: De Mille, R. [Ed.] *The Don Juan Papers: Further Castaneda Controversies*. Ross-Erikson Publishers, Santa Barbara, CA. pp. 94–98.

Centro Espírita Beneficente União do Vegetal 1989. *União do Vegetal: Hoasca. Fundamentos e Objetivos*. Centro de Memória e Documentação, Brasilia, Brasil.

Chango, A. *et al.* 1984. *Yachaj Sami Yachachina*. Colección Mundo Shuar, Quito, Ecuador. Preface by N.E. Whitten, Jr.

Chantre y Herrera, J. 1901. *Historia de las Misiones de la Compañía de Jesús en el Marañón Español... 1637–1767*. Madrid, Spain.

Chen, A.L. and K.K. Chen 1939. "Harmin: The alkaloid of *caapi*" *Quarterly Journal of Pharmacy and Pharmacology* 12: 30–38.

Clinquart, E. 1926. "Contribution à l'étude de la liane Yagé et de son alcaloïde" *Journal de Pharmacie [Belgique]* 36: 671–674.

Cohen, S.I. 1964. *The Beyond Within: The LSD Story*. Atheneum, New York.

Cooke, M.C. 1860. *The Seven Sisters of Sleep. Popular History of the Seven Prevailing Narcotics [sic] of the World*. Blackwell, London, England. Facsimile reprint in 1989, Quarterman Publications Inc., Lincoln, MA.

Cooper, R. [C. Render, Ed.] 1977. *A Guide to British Psilocybin Mushrooms*. Hassle Free Press, London, England. Second edition 1978.

Córdova-Ríos, M. and F.B. Lamb 1971. *Wizard [sic] of the Upper Amazon*. Atheneum, New York. See Lamb 1974.

Corothie, E. and T. Nakano 1969. "Constituents of the bark of *Virola sebifera*" *Planta Medica* 17(2): 184–188.

Costa, O. de A. 1956. "Sobre o identidade botánica do yagé (desfazendo una confusão)" *Revista da Associação Brasileira de Farmácia* 37(11): 481–489.

Cox, P.A. 1991. "Polynesian herbal medicine" In: Cox, P.A. and S.A. Banack [Eds.] *Islands, Plants, and Polynesians: An Introduction to Polynesian Ethnobotany.* Dioscorides Press, Portland, OR. pp. 147–168.

Cuatrecasas, J. 1965. "*Banisteriopsis caapi, B. inebrians, B. rusbyana*" *Journal d'Agriculture Tropicale et de Botanique Appliqueé* 12: 424–429.

Culvenor, C.C.J. *et al.* 1964. "The occurrence of indolealkylamine alkaloids in *Phalaris tuberosa* L. and *P. arundinacea* L." *Australian Journal of Chemistry* 17: 1301–1304.

Dalmer, O. 1929. "Weitere Beitrag zum Identitätsbeweis der Alkaloide Harmin und Banisterin" *Deutscher Medizinischer Wochenschrift* 38: 1592.

Da Mota, C. 1991. *As Jurema Told Us: Kariki Shoko and Shoco Modo of Utilization of Medicinal Plants in the Context of Modern Northeastern Brazil.* Univ. of Mich., Ann Arbor, MI.

Davis, E.W. 1988. *Passage of Darkness: The Ethnobiology of the Haitian Zombie.* Univ. of North Carolina Press, Chapel Hill, NC.

Davis, E.W. and J.A. Yost 1983. "Novel hallucinogens from eastern Ecuador" *Botanical Museum Leaflets* Harvard University 29(3): 291–295.

De Moraes, E.H.F. *et al.* 1990. "As bases nitrogenadas de *Mimosa scabrella* Bentham" *Química Nova* 13(4): 308–309.

Der Marderosian, A.H. *et al.* 1968. "Native use and occurence [*sic*] of N,N-dimethyltryptamine in the leaves of *Banisteriopsis rusbyana*" *American Journal of Pharmacy* 140(5): 137–147.

Der Marderosian, A.H. *et al.* 1970. "The use and hallucinatory [*sic*] principles of a psychoactive beverage of the Cashinahua tribe (Amazon basin)" *Drug Dependence* 5: 7–14.

De Siqueira-Jaccoud, R.J. 1959. "Contribui-ção para o estudo farmacognóstico do *Cabi paraensis* Ducke. I." *Revista da Associação Brasileira de Farmácia* 40(7/8): 75–91.

De Smet, P.A.G.M. 1983. "A multidisciplinary overview of intoxicating enema rituals in the western hemisphere" *Journal of Ethnopharmacology* 9(2,3): 129–166.

De Smet, P.A.G.M. 1985. *Ritual Enemas and Snuffs in the Americas.* Foris Publications, Dordrecht, Netherlands; Cinnaminson, NJ.

Deulofeu, V. 1967. "Chemical components isolated from Banisteriopsis and related species" In: Efron, D.H. *et al.* [Eds.] *Ethnopharmacologic Search for Psychoactive Drugs.* [Public Health Service Publication No. 1645] U.S. Government Printing Office, Washington, D.C. pp. 393–402.

Deulofeu, V. 1973. "Distribution of indolethylamines [*sic*] and β-carbolines in plants" *Ciência e Cultura* 25(7): 649–659.

Díaz, J.L. 1975. "Etnofarmacología de algunos psicotrópicos vegetales de México" *Cuadernos Científicos CEMEF* 4: 135–201.

Dobkin de Ríos, M. 1970a. "Banisteriopsis in witchcraft [*sic*] and healing activities in Iquitos, Peru" *Economic Botany* 24(3): 296–300.

Dobkin de Ríos, M. 1970b. "A note on the use of ayahuasca among urban mestizo populations in the Peruvian Amazon" *American Anthropologist* 72(6): 1419–1422.

Dobkin de Ríos, M. 1972. *Visionary Vine: Hallucinogenic Healing in the Peruvian Amazon.* Chandler Publishing Co., San Francisco, CA.

Dobkin de Ríos, M. 1973. "Curing with *ayahuasca* in an urban slum" In: Harner, M.J. [Ed.] *Hallucinogens and Shamanism.* Oxford Univ. Press, London, England. pp. 67–85.

Dobkin de Ríos, M. 1992. *Amazon Healer: The Life and Times of an Urban Shaman.* Prism Press, Bridport, England.

Doniger O'Flaherty, W. 1982. "Epilogue" *Journal of the American Oriental Society* 102(4): 591–603.

Ducke, A. 1957. "Capí, caapi, cabí, cayahuasca

e yagé" *Revista da Associação Brasileira de Farmácia* 38(12): 283–284.

Elger, F. 1928. "Über das Vorkommen von Harmin in einer südamerikanischen Liane (Yagé)" *Helvetica Chimica Acta* 11: 162–166.

El-Imam, Y.M.A. and **W.C. Evans** 1990. "Alkaloids of a *Datura candida* cultivar, *D. aurea* and various hybrids" *Fitoterapia* 61(2): 148–152.

Emboden, W.A. 1979. *Narcotic Plants.* Second Edition Revised and Enlarged. Macmillan Publishing Co., New York. Orig. 1972.

Escohotado, A. 1989. *Historia General de las Drogas.* Three volumes. Alianza Editorial, Madrid, Spain. Revised edition 1992.

Estrada, A. 1977. *Vida de María Sabina: La Sabia de los Hongos.* Siglo Veintiuno, México City. "Presentación" by R. Gordon Wasson.

Evans, W.C. *et al.* 1965. "The alkaloids of the genus *Datura*, section Brugmansia. Part III. *Datura sanguinea* R. and P." *Planta Medica* 13: 353–358.

Fabing, H.D. and **J.R. Hawkins** 1956. "Intravenous bufotenine injection in the human being" *Science* 123: 886–887.

Fischer, O. 1885. "Über Harmin und Harmalin. II." *Berichte der Deutschen Chemischen Gesellschaft* 18: 400.

Fischer Cárdenas, G. 1923. *Estudio Sobre el Principio Activo del Yagé.* Thesis, Universidad Nacional, Bogotá, Colombia.

Fish, M.S. *et al.* 1955. "Piptadenia alkaloids. Indole bases of *P. peregrina* (L.) Benth. and related species" *Journal of the American Chemical Society* 77: 5892–5895.

Fitzgerald, J.S. and **A.A. Sioumis** 1965. "Alkaloids of the Australian Leguminosae V. The occurrence of methylated tryptamines in Acacia maidenii F. Muell." *Australian Journal of Chemistry* 18: 433–434.

Flores, F.A. and **W.H. Lewis** 1978. "Drinking the South American hallucinogenic ayahuasca" *Economic Botany* 32(2): 154–156.

Frahn, J.L. and **R.J. Illman** 1973. "Separation of some indolylalkylamines from their metho cation derivatives using neutral polystyrene resin" *Journal of Chromatography* 87: 187–191.

Friedberg, C. 1965. "Des *Banisteriopsis* utilsés comme drogue en Amérique du Sud. Essai d'étude critique" *Journal d'Agriculture Tropicale et de Botanique Appliqueé* 12(9-12): 403–437; 550–594; 729–780.

Fritzsche, J. 1847. "Bestandtheile der Samen von *Peganum harmala*" *Justus Liebig's Annalen der Chemie* 64: 360–364.

Furst, P.T. 1976. *Hallucinogens and Culture.* Chandler & Sharp, Novato, CA.

Furst, P.T. and **M.D. Coe** 1977. "Ritual enemas" *Natural History* 86: 88–91.

Gander, J.E. *et al.* 1976. "The occurrence of 2-methyl-1,2,3,4-tetrahydro-β-carboline and variation in alkaloids in *Phalaris arundinacea*" *Phytochemistry* 15: 737–738.

García Barriga, H. 1958. "El yagé, caapi o ayahuasca: Un alucinógeno amazónico" *Revista de la Universidad Nacional de Colombia* 23: 59–76.

García Barriga, H. 1975. *Flora Medicinal de Colombia.* Univ. Nacional, Bogotá, Colombia.

Gartz, J. 1993. *Narrenschwämme: Psychotrope Pilze in Europa—Herausforderung an Forschung und Wertsystem.* Editions Heuwinkel, Basel, Switzerland. Vorwort by C. Rätsch.

Gates, B. 1982. "A monograph of Banisteriopsis and Diplopterys, Malpighiaceae" *Flora Neotropica.* [Monograph No. 30] The New York Botanical Garden, Bronx, NY.

Gates, B. 1986. "La taxonomía de las *malpigiáceas* utilizadas en el brebaje del *ayahuasca*" *América Indígena* 46(1): 49–72.

Gebhart-Sayer, A. 1986. "Una terápia estética. Los diseños visionarios del ayahuasca entre los Shipibo-Conibo" *América Indígena* 46(1): 189–218.

Gelpke, R. 1962. "Von Fahrten in den Weltraum der Seele: Berichte über Selbstversuche mit Delysid (LSD) und Psilocybin (CY)" *Antaios* 3(5): 393–411.

Gelpke, R. 1966. *Vom Rausch im Orient und Okzident.* E. Klett Verlag, Stuttgart, Germany.

Gelpke, R. [Translation by J. Ott] 1981. "On travels in the universe of the soul: Reports on self-experiments with Delysid (LSD) and Psilocybin (CY)" *Journal of Psychoactive Drugs* 13(1): 81–89.

Gershon, S. and **W.J. Lang** 1962. "A psychopharmacological study of some indole alkaloids" *Archives Internationales de Pharmacodynamie et de Thérapie* 135(1-2): 31–56.

Ghosal, S. 1972. "Occurrence of psychodelic substances in some Indian medicinal plants" *Planta Medica* 21(2): 200–209.

Ghosal, S. and **P.K. Banerjee** 1969. "Alkaloids of the roots of *Desmodium gangeticum*" *Australian Journal of Chemistry* 22: 2029–2031.

Ghosal, S. and **S.K. Bhattacharya** 1972. "*Desmodium* alkaloids part II. Chemical and pharmacological evaluation of *D. gangeticum*" *Planta Medica* 22(4): 434–440.

Ghosal, S. and **U.K. Mazumder** 1971. "Malpighiaceae: Alkaloids of the leaves of *Banistereopsis* [sic] *argentea*" *Phytochemistry* 10: 2840–2841.

Ghosal, S. and **B. Mukherjee** 1964. "Alkaloids of *Desmodium pulchellum* Benth. ex Baker" *Journal of the Society of Chemistry and Industry* 1964: 1800.

Ghosal, S. and **B. Mukherjee** 1965. "Occurrence of 5-methoxy-*N,N*-dimethyltryptamine oxide and other tryptamines in *Desmodium pulchellum* Benth ex Baker" *Journal of the Society of Chemistry and Industry* 1965: 793–794.

Ghosal, S. and **B. Mukherjee** 1966. "Indole-3-alkylamine bases of *Desmodium pulchellum*" *Journal of Organic Chemistry* 31: 2284–2288.

Ghosal, S. *et al.* 1969. "*Arundo donax* L. (Graminae). [sic] Phytochemical and pharmacological evaluation" *Journal of Medicinal Chemistry* 12: 480–483.

Ghosal, S. *et al.* 1971a. "Alkaloids of *Desmodium triflorum*" *Phytochemistry* 10: 3312–3313.

Ghosal, S. *et al.* 1971b. "Alkaloids of *Mucuna pruriens* chemistry and pharmacology" *Planta Medica* 19(3): 279–284.

Ghosal, S. *et al.* 1971c. "Chemical and pharmacological evaluation of *Banistereopsis* [sic] *argentea* Spring ex Juss" *Journal of Pharmaceutical Sciences* 60(8): 1209–1212.

Ghosal, S. *et al.* 1972a. "Chemical and pharmacological evaluation of *Desmodium pulchellum*" *Planta Medica* 21(4): 398–409.

Ghosal, S. *et al.* 1972b. "*Desmodium* alkaloids IV. Chemical and pharmacological evaluation of *D. triflorum*" *Planta Medica* 23(4): 321–329.

Ghosal, S. *et al.* 1972c. "Indole bases of *Desmodium gyrans*" *Phytochemistry* 11: 1863–1864.

Ghosal, S. *et al.* 1972d. "Occurrence of curarimimetic indoles in the flowers of *Arundo donax*" *Planta Medica* 21(1): 22–28.

Giove, R. 1992. "Madre Ayahuasca" *Takiwasi* 1: 7–10.

Göbel, H. 1841. *Justus Liebig's Annalen der Chemie* 38: 363.

Goldman, I. 1963. *The Cubeo: Indians of the Northwest Amazon.* [Illinois Studies in Anthropology No. 2] University of Illinois Press, Urbana, IL.

Gonçalves de Lima, O. 1946. "Observações sôbre o 'vinho de Jurema' utilzado pelos índios Pancarú de Tacaratú (Pernambuco)" *Arquivos do Instituto de Pesquisas Agronómicas* 4: 45–80.

Gotu, M. *et al.* 1958. "Studies on useful components of natural sources. XVII. Studies on uterus contracting ingredients in plants. (2). On uterus contracting ingredients in *Lespedeza bicolor* Turcz. var. *japonica* Nakai" *Yakugaku Zasshi* 78(5): 464–467.

Gracie and **Zarkov** 1985. "Three β-carboline containing plants as potentiators of synthetic DMT and other indole psychedelics" *Notes from the Underground* 7: 1–8.

Gracie and **Zarkov** 1986. "An Indo-European

plant teacher" *Notes from the Underground* 10: 1–5.

Greenwood, J. 1993. "Ayahuasca report: An interesting account of the effects of oral DMT/harmaline" *Alt.Drugs* 52992. *Internet* "Sydney University Chemical Mind Control Laboratories," 29 June, 16:31:36 GMT.

Grieg, M.E. *et al.* 1959. "The effect of three tryptamine derivatives on serotonin metabolism *in vitro* and *in vivo*" *Journal of Pharmacology and Experimental Therapeutics* 127: 110–115.

Grina, J.A. *et al.* 1982. "Old and new alkaloids from *Zanthoxylum arborescens*" *Journal of Organic Chemistry* 47(13): 2648–2651.

Gunn, J.A. 1937. "The harmine group of alkaloids" In: Hübner, W. and J. Schüller [Eds.] *Handbuch der Experimentellen Pharmakologie* Volume 5. Springer-Verlag, Berlin, Germany. pp. 184–196.

Haard, R. and **K. Haard** 1975. *Poisonous and Hallucinogenic Mushrooms.* Cloudburst Press, Seattle, WA. Second edition, 1977.

Halpern, L. 1930a. "Der Wirkungsmechanismus des Harmins und der Pathophysiologie der Parkinsonehen Krankheit" *Deutscher Medizinischer Wochenschrift* 56: 651–655.

Halpern, L. 1930b. "Über die Harminwirkung im Selbstversuch" *Deutscher Medizinischer Wochenschrift* 56: 1252–1254.

Hamel, P.B. and **M.U. Chiltoskey** 1975. *Cherokee Plants.* Herald Publishing, Sylva, NC.

Harner, M.J. [Ed.] 1973a. *Hallucinogens and Shamanism.* Oxford University Press, London and Oxford, England and New York.

Harner, M.J. 1973b. "The sound of rushing water" In: Harner, M.J. [Ed.] *Hallucinogens and Shamanism.* Oxford University Press, London, England. pp. 15–27.

Harner, M.J. 1973c. "Common themes in South American Indian *yagé* experiences" In: Harner, M.J. [Ed.] *Hallucinogens and Shamanism.* Oxford University Press, London, England. pp. 155–175.

Harris, B. 1976. *Growing Wild Mushrooms: A Complete Guide to Cultivating Edible and Hallucinogenic Mushrooms.* Wingbow Press, Berkeley, CA. Second edition, 1978.

Harrison, K. 1993. Personal communications, Occidental, CA.

Hashimoto, Y. and **K. Kawanishi** 1975. "New organic bases from Amazonian *Banisteriopsis caapi*" *Phytochemistry* 14: 1633–1635.

Hashimoto, Y. and **K. Kawanishi** 1976. "New alkaloids from *Banisteriopsis caapi*" *Phytochemistry* 15: 1559–1560.

Hassan, I. 1967. "Some folk uses of *Peganum harmala* in India and Pakistan" *Economic Botany* 21(4): 384.

Heffter, A. 1896. "Über Cacteenalkaloïde. (II. Mittheilung)" *Berichte der Deutschen Chemischen Gesellschaft* 29: 216–227.

Heffter, A. 1898. "Über Pellote. Beiträge zur chemischen und pharmakologischen Kenntnis der Cacteen. Zweite Mittheilung" *Naunyn Schmiedeberg's Archiv für Experimentelle Pathologie und Pharmakologie* 40: 385–429.

Henman, A. 1982. "Guaraná (*Paullinia cupana* var. *sorbilis*): Ecological and social perspectives on an economic plant of the central Amazon basin" *Journal of Ethnopharmacology* 6(3): 311–338.

Henman, A. 1986. "Uso del ayahuasca en un contexto autoritario. El caso de la *União do Vegetal* en Brasil" *América Indígena* 46(1): 219–234.

Hernández, F. 1651. *Nova Plantarum, Animalium et Mineralium Mexicanorum Historia.* B. Deversini et Z. Masotti, Rome, Italy.

Hochstein, F.A. and **A.M. Paradies** 1957. "Alkaloids of *Banisteria caapi* and *Prestonia amazonicum* [*sic*]" *Journal of the American Chemical Society* 79: 5735–5736.

Hofmann, A. [Translation by J. Ott] 1980. *LSD: My Problem Child.* McGraw-Hill, New York. From *LSD: Mein Sorgenkind.* Verlag Klett-Cotta, Stuttgart, Germany, 1979. "Translator's Preface" by Jonathan Ott.

Hofmann, A. [Translation by D. Hagenbach] 1989. *Insight Outlook*. Humanics New Age, Atlanta, GA. From *Einsichten Ausblicke*, Sphinx Verlag, Basel, Switzerland, 1986.

Holmstedt, B.R. 1965. "Tryptamine derivatives in epená: An intoxicating snuff used by some South American Indian tribes" *Archives Internationales de Pharmacodynamie et de Thérapie* 156(2): 285–305.

Holmstedt, B.R. and J.-E. Lindgren 1967. "Chemical constituents and pharmacology of South American snuffs" In: Efron, D.H. *et al.* [Eds.] *Ethnopharmacologic Search for Psychoactive Drugs*. [Public Health Service Publication No. 1645] U.S. Government Printing Office, Washington, D.C. pp. 339–373.

Holmstedt, B.R. *et al.* 1971. "Determination of cocaine in some South American species of *Erythroxylum* using mass fragmentography" *Phytochemistry* 16: 1753–1755.

Holmstedt, B.R. *et al.* 1978. "Cocaine in blood of coca chewers" *Botanical Museum Leaflets* Harvard University 26(5): 199–201.

Holmstedt, B.R. *et al.* 1980. "Indole alkaloids in Amazonian Myristicaceae: Field and laboratory research" *Botanical Museum Leaflets* Harvard University 28(3): 215–234.

Horowitz, M. 1991. "Just say know: Gordon Wasson and the Psychedelic [sic] Revolution" *Integration: Zeitschrift für Geistbewegende Pflanzen und Kultur* 1: 4–6.

Hsu, H.-Y. 1970. *Abstract of the Annual Meeting of the Association of Pharmacology*. The China Academy, Beijing, China.

Hugh-Jones, S. 1979. *The Palm and the Pleiades: Initiation and Cosmology in the Northwest Amazonia*. Cambridge University Press, Cambridge, England.

Iacobucci, G.A. and E.A. Rúveda 1964. "Bases derived from tryptamine in Argentine *Piptadenia* species" *Phytochemistry* 3: 465–467.

Iyer, V.V.S. and R. Robinson 1934. *Journal of the Chemical Society* 1934: 1635.

Jiménez de la Espada, M. 1889. *Relaciones Geográficas de Indias: Perú*. Ministerio de Fomento, Madrid, Spain.

Johns, S.R. *et al.* 1966. "Alkaloids of the Australian Leguminosae VI. Alkaloids of *Petalostylis labicheoides* var. *casseoides* Benth." *Australian Journal of Chemistry* 19: 893.

Johnston, J.F. 1853–1855. *The Chemistry of Common Life*. Two volumes. D. Appleton & Co., New York [Ninth Edition, 1857].

Joyal, E. 1987. "Ethnobotanical field notes from Ecuador: Camp, Prieto, Jørgensen, and Giler" *Economic Botany* 41(2): 163–189.

Jünger, E. 1970. *Annäherungen: Drogen und Rausch*. Ernst Klett Verlag, Stuttgart, Germany. Spanish translation, 1993.

Kan-Fan, C. *et al.* 1970. "Alcaloïdes de *Vepris ampody* (Rutacées)" *Phytochemistry* 9: 1283–1291.

Kawanishi, K. *et al.* 1982. "Shihunine and dihydroshihunine from *Banisteriopsis caapi*" *Journal of Natural Products* 45: 637–639.

Keller, O. and F. Gottauf 1929. "Über einige im Heimatlande arzneilich benutzte bolivianische Drogen. I. Chemische Untersuchung" *Archiv der Pharmazie und Berichte der Deutschen Pharmazeutischen Gesellschaft* 267: 373–390.

Kensinger, K.M. 1973. "*Banisteriopsis* usage among the Peruvian Cashinahua" In: Harner, M.J. [Ed.] *Hallucinogens and Shamanism*. Oxford University Press, London and Oxford, England and New York. pp. 9–14.

Kobilková, Z. and J. Trojánek 1966. "The absolute configuration of (+)-1,2,3,4-tetrahydroharmine" *Journal of the Society of Chemistry and Industry* 1966: 1342.

Koch-Grünberg, T. 1909–1910. *Zwei Jahre unter den Indianern. Reisen in Nordwest-Brasilien 1903/1905*. Two volumes. Ernst Wasmuth, Berlin, Germany.

Koch-Grünberg, T. 1923. *Von Roraima zum Orinoco*. Volume 3. Verlag Stecker und Schröder, Stuttgart, Germany.

Kohn, E.O. 1992. "Some observations on the

use of medicinal plants from primary and secondary growth by the Runa of eastern lowland Ecuador" *Journal of Ethnobiology* 12(1): 141–152.

Kusel, H. 1965. "Ayahuasca drinkers among the Chama Indians of Northeast Peru" *Psychedelic Review* 6: 58-66.

Lamb, F.B. 1974. *Wizard[sic] of the Upper Amazon: The Story of Manuel Córdova-Ríos.* Houghton-Mifflin, Boston, MA. Introduction by Andrew T. Weil.

Lamb, F.B. 1981a. "Comment on Bock's review of *The Don Juan Papers*" *American Anthropologist* 88(3): 641.

Lamb, F.B. 1981b. *"Wizard of the Upper Amazon* as Ethnography" *Current Anthropology* 22(5): 577–580.

Langdon, E.J. 1986. "Las clasificaciones del yajé dentro del grupo Siona: Etnobotánica, etnoquímica e historia" *América Indígena* 46(1): 101–116.

Lebœuf, M. *et al.* 1977. "Alcaloïdes et triterpènes du *Testulea gabonensis* Pellegr." *Plantes Médicinales et Phytothérapie* 11: 230–235.

Lee, M.A. and B. Shlain 1985. *Acid Dreams: LSD, the CIA and the Sixties Rebellion.* Grove Press, Inc. New York.

Legler, G. and R. Tschesche 1963. "Die Isolierung von N-Methyltryptamin, 5-Methoxy-N-methyltryptamin und 5-Methoxy-N,N-dimethyltryptamin aus der Rinde von Piptadenia peregrina Benth." *Die Naturwißenschaften* 50: 94–95.

León Portilla, M. 1961. *Los Antiguos Mexicanos.* Fondo de Cultura Económica, México City.

Leuner, H. and M. Schlichtung [Translation by J. Baker] 1989. "A report on the symposium 'On the Current State of Research in the Area of Psychoactive Substances'" In: Rätsch, C. [Ed.] *Gateway to Inner Space: Sacred Plants, Mysticism and Psychotherapy–A Festschrift in Honor of Albert Hofmann.* Prism Press, Bridport, England. pp. 213–240.

Levy, S. 1991. "Search and destroy: What happened when the Secret Service visited Steve Jackson Games" *Macworld.* March issue, pp. 51 *et seq.*

Lewin, L. 1888. "Über *Anhalonium lewinii*" *Naunyn Schmiedeberg's Archiv für Experimentelle Pathologie und Pharmakologie* 24: 401–411.

Lewin, L. 1924. *Phantastica—Die Betäubenden und Erregenden Genußmittel. Für Ärzte und Nichtärzte.* Verlag von Georg Stilke, Berlin, Germany. English editions 1931, 1964.

Lewin, L. 1928. "Untersuchungen über *Banisteria caapi* Spr. (ein südamerikanisches Rauschmittel)" *Naunyn Schmiedeberg's Archiv für Experimentelle Pathologie und Pharmakologie* 129: 133–149.

Lewin, L. 1929. *Banisteria caapi: Ein Neues Rauschgift [sic] und Heilmittel.* Verlag von Georg Stilke, Berlin, Germany.

Lewin, L. and P. Schuster 1929. "Ergebnisse von Banisterinversuchen an Kranken" *Deutscher Medizinischer Wochenschrift* 55: 419.

Lewis, W.H. *et al.* 1991. "Ritualistic use of the holly *Ilex guayusa* by Amazonian Jívaro [sic] Indians" *Journal of Ethnopharmacology* 33(1,2): 25–30.

Lipp. F.J. 1990. "Mixe concepts and uses of entheogenic mushrooms" In: Riedlinger, T.J. [Ed.] *The Sacred Mushroom Seeker: Essays for R. Gordon Wasson.* [Ethnomycological Studies No. 11] Dioscorides Press, Portland, OR. pp. 151–159.

Lipp. F.J. 1991. *The Mixe of Oaxaca: Religion, Ritual and Healing.* University of Texas Press, Austin, TX. Foreword by M.S. Edmondson.

Liwszyc, G.E. *et al.* 1992. "Daime—A ritual herbal potion" *Journal of Ethnopharmacology* 36(1): 91–92.

Lockwood, T.E. 1979. "The ethnobotany of *Brugmansia*" *Journal of Ethnopharmacology* 1(2): 147–164.

Lowie, R.H. 1946. "The indians of eastern Brazil. Eastern Brazil: An introduction" In: Steward, J.H. [Ed.] *Handbook of South American Indians.* [Bureau of American Ethnology Bulletin No. 143] U.S. Government Printing Office, Washington, D.C. pp. 381–397.

Lowy, B. 1987. "Caapi revisited—In Christianity" *Economic Botany* 41(3): 450–452.

Luna, L.E. 1984a. "The healing practices of a Peruvian shaman" *Journal of Ethnopharmacology* 11(2): 123–133.

Luna, L.E. 1984b. "The concept of plants as teachers among four mestizo shamans of Iquitos, northeastern Peru" *Journal of Ethnopharmacology* 11(2): 135–156.

Luna, L.E. 1986a. "Bibliografía sobre el ayahuasca" *América Indígena* 46(1): 235–245.

Luna, L.E. 1986b. "Apéndices" *América Indígena* 46(1): 247–251.

Luna, L.E. 1986c. *Vegetalismo: Shamanism among the Mestizo Population of the Peruvian Amazon.* [Acta Universitatis Stockholmensis, Stockholm Studies in Comparative Religion No. 27] Almqvist and Wiksell International, Stockholm, Sweden.

Luna, L.E. 1991. "Plant spirits in ayahuasca visions by Peruvian painter, Pablo Amaringo. An iconographic analysis" *Integration: Zeitschrift für Geistbewegende Pflanzen und Kultur* 1: 18–29.

Luna, L.E. 1992. Personal communications, San Luis Potosí, México.

Luna, L.E. 1993. Personal communications, Madrid and Huelva, Spain.

Luna, L.E. and P. Amaringo 1991. *Ayahuasca Visions: The Religious Iconography of a Peruvian Shaman.* North Atlantic Books, Berkeley, CA.

Ma, W.W. *et al.* 1986. "Cactus alkaloids, LXI. Identification of mescaline and related compounds in eight additional species using TLC and MS/MS" *Journal of Natural Products* 49(4): 735–737.

McIsaac, W.M. and V. Estévez 1966. "Structure-action relationship of β-carbolines as monoamine oxidase inhibitors" *Biochemical Pharmacology* 15: 1625–1627.

McKenna, D.J. 1992. Personal communications, San Luis Potosí, México.

McKenna, D.J. 1993. "A multinational, interdisciplinary biomedical investigation of hoasca, a plant hallucinogen used in Brazil" *MAPS* 4(2): 27.

McKenna, D.J. and T.K. McKenna 1975. *The Invisible Landscape: Mind, Hallucinogens and the I Ching.* Seabury Press, New York.

McKenna, D.J. and G.H.N. Towers 1984. "Biochemistry and pharmacology of tryptamines and beta-carbolines: A minireview" *Journal of Psychoactive Drugs* 16(4): 347–358.

McKenna, D.J. *et al.* 1984a. "Monoamine oxidase inhibitors in South American hallucinogenic plants: Tryptamine and β-carboline constituents of *ayahuasca*" *Journal of Ethnopharmacology* 10(2): 195–223.

McKenna, D.J. *et al.* 1984b. "Monoamine oxidase inhibitors in South American hallucinogenic plants Part 2: Constituents of orally-active myristicaceous hallucinogens" *Journal of Ethnopharmacology* 12(2): 179–211.

McKenna, D.J. *et al.* 1986. "Ingredientes biodinámicos en las plantas que se mezclan al ayahuasca. Una farmacopea tradicional no investigada" *América Indígena* 46(1): 73–99.

MacRae, E. 1992. *Guiado Pela Lua: Xamanismo e Uso Ritual da Ayahuasca no Culto do Santo Daime.* Editora Brasiliense, São Paolo, Brasil. With "Anexo" of 12 hymns.

Magnin, J. 1740. *Breve Descripción de la Provincia de Quito, y de sus Misiones de Sucumbíos de Religiosos de S. Franco. y de Maynas de Pp. de la Compa. de Jhs. a las Orillas del Gran Río Marañón.* Quito, Ecuador.

Manske, R.H.F. 1931. "A synthesis of the methyl-tryptamines and some derivatives" *Canadian Journal of Research* 5: 592–600.

Manske, R.H.F. *et al.* 1927. "Harmine and harmaline. Part IX. A synthesis of harmaline"

Journal of the Chemical Society (Organic) 1927: 1–15.

Marks, J. 1979. *The Search for the "Manchurian Candidate."* Dell Books, New York.

Marles, R.J. *et al.* 1988. "A contribution to the ethnopharmacology of the lowland Quichua people of Amazonian Ecuador" *Revista de la Academia Colombiana de Ciencias Exactas, Físicas y Naturales* 16(63): 111–120.

Marnell, T. [Ed.] 1993. *Drug Identification Bible.* Drug Identification Bible, Denver, CO.

Marten, G.C. *et al.* 1973. "Alkaloids and palatability of *Phalaris arundinacea* L. grown in diverse environments" *Agronomy Journal* 65: 199–201.

Meckes-Lozoya, M. *et al.* 1990. "N,N-Dimethyltryptamine alkaloid in *Mimosa-tenuiflora* bark (tepescohuite)" *Archivos de Investigación Médica* 21(2): 175–177.

Menser, G.P. 1977. *Hallucinogenic and Poisonous Mushroom Field Guide.* And/Or Press, Berkeley, CA.

Michiels, M. and E. Clinquart 1926. "Sur les réactions chimiques d'identification de la yagéine" *Bulletin de l'Académie Royale du Médecine du Belgique* 5-6: 19–29.

Miller, J.S. 1993. Personal communications, Catemaco and Xalapa, Veracruz, México.

Monardes, N. [E. Denot & S. Satanowsky, Eds.] 1990. *Herbolaria de Indias.* Redacta, México City. "Presentación" by X. Lozoya.

Montgomery, R. 1992. Personal communications, Sebastopol, CA and Maui, HI.

Moore, M. 1989. *Medicinal Plants of the Desert and Canyon West.* Museum of New Mexico Press, Santa Fé, NM. Preface by A. Weil.

Moore, R.M. *et al.* 1967. "Factors affecting concentrations of dimethylated indolealkylamines in *Phalaris tuberosa* L." *Australian Journal of Biological Sciences* 20:1131–1140.

Morimoto, H. and H. Matsumoto 1966. "Über Alkaloide, VI: Inhaltßtoffe von *Lespedeza bicolor* var. *japonica*, II" *Justus Liebig's Annalen der Chemie* 692: 194–199.

Morimoto, H. and H. Oshio 1965. "Über Alkaloide, V: Inhaltßtoffe von *Lespedeza bicolor* var. *japonica*, I. Über Lespedamin, ein neues Alkaloid" *Justus Liebig's Annalen der Chemie* 682: 212–218.

Mors, W.B. and O. Ribeiro 1957. "Occurrence of scopoletin in the genus *Brunfelsia*" *Journal of Organic Chemistry* 22: 978–979.

Mors, W.B. and P. Zaltzman 1954. "Sôbre o alcaloide da *Banisteria caapi* Spruce e do *Cabi paraensis* Ducke" *Boletím do Instituto de Química Agrícola* 34: 17–27.

Morton, C.V. 1931. "Notes on *yagé*, a drug-plant of southeastern Colombia" *Journal of the Washington Academy of Sciences* 21: 485–488.

Mulvena, D.P. and M. Slaytor 1982. "Separation of tryptophan derivatives in *Phalaris aquatica* by thin-layer chromatography" *Journal of Chromatography* 245: 155–157.

Naranjo, C. 1967. "Psychotropic properties of the harmala alkaloids" In: Efron, D.H. *et al.* [Eds.] *Ethnopharmacologic Search for Psychoactive Drugs.* [Public Health Service Publication No. 1645] U.S. Government Printing Office, Washington, D.C. pp. 385–391.

Naranjo, C. 1973. "Psychological aspects of the *yagé* [*sic*] experience in an experimental setting" In: Harner, M.J. [Ed.] *Hallucinogens and Shamanism.* Oxford University Press, London, England. pp. 176–190.

Naranjo, P. 1975. "Drogas psiquedélicas [*sic*] en medicina mágica" *Cuadernos Científicos CEMEF* 4: 73–92.

Naranjo, P. 1979. "Hallucinogenic plant use and related indigenous belief systems in the Ecuadorian Amazon" *Journal of Ethnopharmacology* 1(2): 121–145.

Naranjo, P. 1983. *Ayahuasca: Etnomedicina y Mitología.* Eds. Libri Mundi, Quito, Ecuador.

Naranjo, P. 1986. "El *ayahuasca* en la arqueología ecuatoriana" *América Indígena* 46(1): 117–127.

Nicholson, M.S. and C.B. Arzeni 1993. "The market medicinal plants of Monterrey, Nuevo León, México" *Economic Botany* 47(2): 184–192.

O'Connell, F.D. and E.V. Lynn 1953. "The alkaloid of *Banisteriopsis inebrians* Morton" *Journal of the American Pharmaceutical Association* 42: 753–754.

Oga, S. *et al.* 1984. "Pharmacological trials of crude extract of *Passiflora alata*" *Planta Medica* 50: 303–306.

Oram, R.N. and J.D. Williams 1967. "Variation in concentration and composition of toxic alkaloids among strains of *Phalaris tuberosa* L." *Nature* 213: 946–947.

Ortíz de Montellano, B.R. 1990. *Aztec Medicine, Health, and Nutrition.* Rutgers University Press, New Brunswick, NJ.

Oss, O.T. and O.N. Oeric, with I.T. Obscure and Kat [Pseudonyms for J.E. Bigwood, K. Harrison, D.J. McKenna and T.K. McKenna] 1975. *Psilocybin: Magic Mushroom Grower's Guide.* And/Or Press, Berkeley, CA.

Ott, J. 1975. "Notes on recreational use of hallucinogenic mushrooms" *Boletín de la Sociedad Mexicana de Micología* 9: 131–135.

Ott, J. 1976. *Hallucinogenic Plants of North America.* Wingbow Press, Berkeley, CA. Revised edition 1979. Introduction by Richard Evans Schultes.

Ott, J. 1978. "Recreational use of hallucinogenic mushrooms in the United States" In: Rumack, B.H. and E. Salzman [Eds.] *Mushroom Poisoning: Diagnosis and Treatment.* CRC Press, West Palm Beach, FL. pp. 231–243.

Ott, J. 1985. *The Cacahuatl Eater: Ruminations of an Unabashed Chocolate Addict.* Natural Products Co., Vashon, WA.

Ott, J. 1990. "A twentieth century Darwin" In: Riedlinger, T.J. [Ed.] *The Sacred Mushroom Seeker: Essays for R. Gordon Wasson.* [Ethnomycological Studies No. 11] Dioscorides Press, Portland, OR. pp. 183–191.

Ott, J. 1993. *Pharmacotheon: Entheogenic Drugs, Their Plant Sources and History.* Na-

tural Products Company, Kennewick, WA. Foreword by Albert Hofmann.

Ott, J. In preparation. *Pharmacotheon II: Entheogenic Plants and the Origins of Religions.* Natural Products Co., Kennewick, WA.

Ott, J. and J.E. Bigwood [Eds.] 1978. *Teonanácatl: Hallucinogenic Mushrooms of North America.* Madrona Publishers, Seattle, WA.

Ott, J. and J.E. Bigwood [Eds.; Translation by M.S. Antolín] 1985. *Teonanácatl: Hongos Alucinógenos de Europa y América del Norte.* Editorial Swan, San Lorenzo de El Escorial, Spain. Addenda by D. Belmonte.

Ott, J. and R.G. Wasson 1983. "Carved 'disembodied eyes' of Teotihuacan" *Botanical Museum Leaflets* Harvard University 29(4): 387–400.

Pachter, I.J. *et al.* 1959. "Indole alkaloids of *Acer saccharinum* (the silver maple), *Dictyoloma incanescens, Piptadenia colubrina,* and *Mimosa hostilis*" *Journal of Organic Chemistry* 24: 1285–1287.

Padoch, C. and W. De Jong 1991. "The house gardens of Santa Rosa: Diversity and variability in an Amazonian agricultural system" *Economic Botany* 45(2): 166–175.

Pardanani, J.H. *et al.* 1978. "Cactus alkaloids. XXXVII. Mescaline and related compounds from *Opuntia spinosior*" *Lloydia* 41(3): 286–288.

Paris, R.R. *et al.* 1955. *Comptes Rendus Hebdomadaire des Séances de l'Académie des Sciences* 241: 241.

Paris, R.R. *et al.* 1957. "Alcaloïdes du *Leptactinia densiflora* Hook. f." *Bulletin de la Société Chimique du France* 1957: 780–782.

Pennes, H.H. and P.H. Hoch 1957. "Psychotomimetics [*sic*], clinical and theoretical considerations: Harmine, WIN-2299 and nalline" *American Journal of Psychiatry* 113: 887–892.

Perkin, W.H. and R. Robinson 1919a. "Harmine and harmaline. Part III." *Journal of the Chemical Society (Organic)* 115: 933–967.

Perkin, W.H. and R. Robinson 1919b. "Harmine and harmaline. Part IV." *Journal of the Chemical Society (Organic)* 115: 967–972.

Perrot, E. and Raymond-Hamet 1927a. "Le yagé, plante sensorielle des indiens de la région amazonienne de l'Equateur et de la Colombie" *Comptes Rendus Hebdomadaires des Séances de l'Académie des Sciences* 184: 1266–1268.

Perrot, E. and Raymond-Hamet 1927b. "Yagé, ayahuasca, caapi et leur alcaloïde, télépatheine ou yagéine" *Bulletin des Sciences Pharmacologiques* 34: 337–347; 417–426; 500–514.

Pinkley, H.V. 1969. "Plant admixtures to *ayahuasca*, the South American hallucinogenic drink" *Lloydia* 32(3): 305–314.

Pletscher, A. *et al.* 1959. "Über pharmakologische Beeinflußung des Zentralnervensystems durch kurzwirkende Monoaminoxidasehemmer aus der Gruppe der Harmala-Alkaloide" *Helvetica Physiologica et Pharmacologica Acta* 17: 202–214.

Plowman, T.C. 1977. "Brunfelsia in ethnomedicine" *Botanical Museum Leaflets* Harvard University 25(10): 289–320.

Plowman, T.C. 1981. "Amazonian coca" *Journal of Ethnopharmacology* 3(2&3): 195–225.

Poisson, J. 1965. "Note sur le 'Natem', boisson toxique péruvienne et ses alcaloïdes" *Annales Pharmaceutiques Françaises* 23(4): 241–244.

Polia, M. and A. Bianchi 1993. "The plant teachers of northern Peruvian Andean healers: Ethnobotanical and ethnomedical data" In press, in *Integration: Zeitschrift für Geistbewegende Pflanzen und Kultur* No. 5.

Poupat, C. *et al.* 1976. "Alcaloïdes de *Acacia simplicifolia*" *Phytochemistry* 15: 2019–2020.

Power, F.B. and V.K. Chestnut 1919. "*Ilex vomitoria* as a native source of caffeine" *Journal of the American Chemical Society* 41: 1307–1312.

Prance, G.T. 1970. "Notes on the use of plant hallucinogens in Amazonian Brazil" *Economic Botany* 24(1): 62–68.

Prance, G.T. and J.A. Kallunki [Eds.]1984. *Ethnobotany in the Neotropics.* The New York Botanical Garden, Bronx, NY.

Prance, G.T. and A.E. Prance 1970. "Hallucinations in Amazonia" *Garden Journal* 20: 102–107.

Prance, G.T. *et al.* 1977. "The ethnobotany of the Paumarí Indians" *Economic Botany* 31(2): 129–139.

Ramírez de Jara, M.C. and C.E. Pinzón C. 1986. "Los hijos del bejuco solar y la campana celeste. El yajé en la cultura popular urbana" *América Indígena* 46(1): 163–188.

Ratcliffe, B. 1973. "Psilocybin demand creates new drug deception" *The Pharm Chem Newsletter* 2(2): 1 *et seq.*

Raymond-Hamet, 1941. "Sur les effets vasculaires de l'harmine, de l'harmaline et de la tétrahydroharmine" *Comptes Rendus Hebdomadaires des Séances de la Société de Biologie et de ses Filiales* 135: 69–73.

Reichel-Dolmatoff, G. 1944. "La cultura material de los Indios Guahibo" *Revista del Instituto Etnológico Nacional* 1(1): 437–506.

Reichel-Dolmatoff, G. 1960. "Notas etnográficas sobre los Indios del Chocó" *Revista Colombiana de Antropología* 11: 75–158.

Reichel-Dolmatoff, G. 1969. "El contexto cultural de un alucinógeno aborígen" *Revista de la Academia Colombiana de Ciencias Exactas, Físicas y Naturales* 13(51): 327–345. English version, Reichel-Dolmatoff 1972.

Reichel-Dolmatoff, G. 1970. "Notes on the cultural extent of the use of yajé (*Banisteriopsis caapi*) among the Indians of the Vaupés, Colombia" *Economic Botany* 24(1): 32–33.

Reichel-Dolmatoff, G. 1971. *Amazonian Cosmos: The Sexual and Religious Symbolism of the Tukano Indians.* University of Chicago Press, Chicago, IL.

Reichel-Dolmatoff, G. 1972. "The cultural

context of an aboriginal hallucinogen: *Banisteriopsis caapi* " In: Furst, P.T. [Ed.] *Flesh of the Gods: The Ritual Use of Hallucinogens.* Praeger Publishers, New York. pp. 84–113.

Reichel-Dolmatoff, G. 1975. *The Shaman and the Jaguar: A Study of Narcotic [sic] Drugs Among the Indians of Colombia.* Temple University Press, Philadelphia, PA. Foreword by Richard Evans Schultes.

Reichel-Dolmatoff, G. 1978. *Beyond the Milky Way: Hallucinatory Imagery of the Tukano Indians.* [Latin American Center Publications, UCLA Latin American Studies Vol. 42] University of California Press, Los Angeles, CA.

Reis Altschul, S. von 1967. "Vilca and its use" In: Efron, D.H. *et al.* [Eds.] *Ethnopharmacologic Search for Psychoactive Drugs.* [Public Health Service Publication No. 1645] U.S. Government Printing Office, Washington, D.C. pp. 307–314.

Reis Altschul, S. von 1972. *The Genus Anadenanthera in Amerindian Cultures.* Botanical Museum of Harvard University, Cambridge, MA.

Rivera, A. *et al.* 1989. "*Brugmansia sanguinea* subsp. *vulcanicola*, a good source of scopolamine" *Fitoterapia* 60(6): 542–544.

Rivier, L. and J.-E. Lindgren 1972. "'Ayahuasca,' the South American hallucinogenic drink: An ethnobotanical and chemical investigation" *Economic Botany* 26(1): 101–129.

Rivier, L. and P.-É. Pilet 1971. "Composés hallucinogènes indoliques naturels" *Année Biologique* 10(3-4): 129–149.

Rodríguez, E. *et al.* 1982. "The possible role of Amazonian psychoactive plants in the chemotherapy of parasitic worms—A hypothesis" *Journal of Ethnopharmacology* 6(3): 303–309.

Rouhier, A. 1924. "Le *yagé*: Plante télépathique" *Paris Médical* 52: 341.

Rouhier, A. 1926. "Documents pour serv-

ir à l'étude du yagé" *Bulletin des Sciences Pharmacologiques* 33: 252–261.

Rouhier, A. 1927. *La Plante qui Fait les Yeux Émerveillés—le Peyotl.* Gaston Doin et Cie., Paris, France. Préface by E. Perrot, pp. v.–xii.

Rovelli, B. and G.N. Vaughan 1967. "Alkaloids of *Acacia* I. $N_b N_b$-Dimethyltryptamine in *Acacia phlebophylla* F. Muell." *Australian Journal of Chemistry* 20: 1299–1300.

Ruck, C.A.P. *et al.* 1979. "Entheogens" *Journal of Psychedelic Drugs* 11(1-2): 145–146.

Rusby, H.H. 1923. "The aboriginal uses of *caapi*" *Journal of the American Pharmaceutical Association* 12: 1123.

Russo, E.B. 1992. "Headache treatments by native peoples of the Ecuadorian Amazon: A preliminary cross-disciplinary assessment" *Journal of Ethnopharmacology* 36(3): 193–206.

Sai-Halász, A. 1962. "The effect of antiserotonin on the experimental psychosis [sic] induced by dimethyltryptamine" *Experientia* 18(3): 137–138.

Sai-Halász, A. 1963. "The effect of MAO inhibition on the experimental psychosis [sic] induced by dimethyltryptamine" *Psychopharmacologia* 4(6): 385–388.

Sai-Halász, A. *et al.* 1958. "Dimethyltryptamin: Ein neues Psychoticum [sic]" *Psychiatria et Neurologia* [Basel] 135: 285–301.

Samorini, G. 1992. Personal communications, San Luis Potosí and Xalapa, México.

Schmeda Hirschmann, G. and A.R. De Arias 1990. "A survey of medicinal plants of Minas Gerais, Brazil" *Journal of Ethnopharmacology* 29(2): 159–172.

Schroeder, D.R. 1986(5). "Isolation and biomimetic synthesis of bishordeninyl terpene alkaloids from *Zanthoxylum procerum*" *Dissertation Abstracts International* 47(2): 636–B.

Schultes, R.E. 1942. "Plantae Colombianae II. Yoco: A stimulant of southern Colombia" *Botanical Museum Leaflets* Harvard University 10(10): 301–324.

Schultes, R.E. 1954a. "Plantae Austro-Americanae IX. Plantarum novarum vel notabilium notae diversae" *Botanical Museum Leaflets* Harvard University 16(8): 179–228.

Schultes, R.E. 1954b. "A new narcotic [*sic*] snuff from the northwest Amazon" *Botanical Museum Leaflets* Harvard University 16(9): 241–260.

Schultes, R.E. 1957. "The identity of the malpighiaceous narcotics [*sic*] of South America" *Botanical Museum Leaflets* Harvard University 18(1): 1–56.

Schultes, R.E. 1960. "A reputedly toxic *Malouetia* from the Amazon" *Botanical Museum Leaflets* Harvard University 19(5): 123–124.

Schultes, R.E. 1969a. "De plantis toxicariis e mundo novo tropicale commentationes IV" *Botanical Museum Leaflets* Harvard University 22(4): 133–164.

Schultes, R.E. 1969b. "De plantis toxicariis e mundo novo tropicale commentationes V. *Virola* as an orally administered hallucinogen" *Botanical Museum Leaflets* Harvard University 22(6): 229–240.

Schultes, R.E. 1972a. "De plantis toxicariis e mundo novo tropicale commentationes X. New data on the malpighiaceous narcotics [*sic*] of South America" *Botanical Museum Leaflets* Harvard University 23(3): 137–147.

Schultes, R.E. [S.H. Wassén, Ed.] 1972b. "*Ilex guayusa* from 500 A.D. to the present" *Göteborgs Etnografiska Museum Etnologiska Studier* 32: 115–138.

Schultes, R.E. 1975. "De plantis toxicariis e mundo novo tropicale commentationes XIII. Notes on poisonous or medicinal malpighiaceous species of the Amazon" *Botanical Museum Leaflets* Harvard University 24(6): 121–131.

Schultes, R.E. 1977. "A new hallucinogen from Andean Colombia: *Iochroma fuchsioides*" *Journal of Psychedelic Drugs* 9(1): 45–49.

Schultes, R.E. [J. Ott, Ed.] 1979a. "Evolution of the identification of the major South American narcotic [*sic*] plants" *Journal of Psychedelic Drugs* 11(1-2): 119–134.

Schultes, R.E. 1979b. "Discovery of an ancient guayusa plantation in Colombia" *Botanical Museum Leaflets* Harvard University 27(5-6): 143–153.

Schultes, R.E. 1981. "Coca in the northwest Amazon" *Journal of Ethnopharmacology* 3(2&3): 173–194.

Schultes, R.E. 1983. "De plantis toxicariis e mundo novo tropicale commentationes XXXIII. Ethnobotanical, floristic and nomenclatural notes on plants of the northwest Amazon" *Botanical Museum Leaflets* Harvard University 29(4): 343–365.

Schultes, R.E. 1985a. "De plantis toxicariis e mundo novo tropicale commentationes XXXIV: Biodynamic rubiaceous plants of the northwest Amazon" *Journal of Ethnopharmacology* 14(2,3): 105–124.

Schultes, R.E. 1985b. "De plantis toxicariis e mundo novo tropicale commentationes XXXVI. A novel method of utilizing the hallucinogenic Banisteriopsis" *Botanical Museum Leaflets* Harvard University 30(3): 61–63.

Schultes, R.E. 1986a. "Recognition of variability in wild plants by Indians of the northwest Amazon: An enigma" *Journal of Ethnobiology* 6(2): 229–238.

Schultes, R.E. 1986b. "El desarrollo histórico de la identificación de las malpigiáceas empleadas como alucinógenos" *América Indígena* 46(1): 9–47.

Schultes, R.E. 1987. "A caffeine drink prepared from bark" *Economic Botany* 41(4): 526–527.

Schultes, R.E. 1988. *Where the Gods Reign:*

Plants and Peoples of the Colombian Amazon. Synergetic Press, Oracle, AZ.

Schultes, R.E. and A. Hofmann 1979. *Plants of the Gods: Origins of Hallucinogenic Use*. McGraw-Hill, New York. 1992 reprint, Healing Arts Press, Rochester, VT.

Schultes, R.E. and A. Hofmann 1980. *The Botany and Chemistry of Hallucinogens*. Enlarged Second Edition. C.C. Thomas, Springfield, IL. Foreword by H. Klüver.

Schultes, R.E. and B.R. Holmstedt 1968. "De plantis toxicariis e mundo novo tropicale commentationes II. The vegetal ingredients of the myristicaceous snuffs of the northwest Amazon" *Rhodora* 70: 113–160.

Schultes, R.E. and R.F. Raffauf 1960. "Prestonia: An Amazon narcotic [*sic*] or not?" *Botanical Museum Leaflets* Harvard University 19(5): 109–122.

Schultes, R.E. and R.F. Raffauf 1990. *The Healing Forest: Medicinal and Toxic Plants of the Northwest Amazonia*. Dioscorides Press, Portland, OR. Foreword by H.R.H. Philip.

Schultes, R.E. and R.F. Raffauf 1992. *Vine of the Soul: Medicine Men, Their Plants and Rituals in the Colombian Amazon*. Synergetic Press, Oracle, AZ. Foreword G.T. Prance.

Schultes, R.E. and T. Swain 1976. "De plantis toxicariis e mundo novo tropicale commentationes XIII. Further notes on Virola as an orally administered hallucinogen" *Journal of Psychedelic Drugs* 8(4): 317–324.

Schultes, R.E. *et al.* 1969. "De plantis toxicariis e mundo novo tropicale commentationes III. Phytochemical examination of Spruce's original collection of Banisteriopsis caapi" *Botanical Museum Leaflets* Harvard University 22(4): 121–132.

Schultes, R.E. *et al.* 1977. "De plantis toxicariis e mundo novo tropicale commentationes XVII. *Virola* as an oral hallucinogen among the Boras of Peru" *Botanical Museum Leaflets* Harvard University 25(9): 259–272.

Seil, H. and E. Putt 1924. "The chemical examination of *caapi*: A preliminary report" *Journal of the American Pharmaceutical Association* 13: 99–101.

Shemluck, M.J. 1979. "The flowers of Ilex guayusa" *Botanical Museum Leaflets* Harvard University 27(5-6): 155–160.

Shulgin, A.T. 1976. "Profiles of psychedelic drugs. 1. DMT" *Journal of Psychedelic Drugs* 8(2): 167–168.

Shulgin, A.T. 1993. Personal communications, Maui, HI and Madrid, Spain.

Shulgin, A.T. and A. Shulgin 1991. *PIHKAL: A Chemical Love Story*. Transform Press, Berkeley, CA. Foreword by D.E. Nichols.

Shulgin, A.T. and A. Shulgin 1994. *TIHKAL*. Transform Press, Berkeley, CA, in preparation.

Siskind, J. 1973. "Visions and cures among the Sharanahua" In: Harner, M.J. [Ed.] *Hallucinogens and Shamanism*. Oxford University Press, London and Oxford, England and New York. pp. 28–39.

Skaltsounis, A.L. *et al.* 1983. "Plantes de Nouvelle-Calédonie. LXXXIII. Alcaloïdes des tiges feuillées de *Melicope leptococca*" *Journal of Natural Products* 46(5): 732–735.

Smith, T.A. 1977. "Tryptamine and related compounds in plants" *Phytochemistry* 16: 171–175.

Späth, E. and E. Lederer 1930a. "Synthese der Harmala-Alkaloide: Harmalin, Harmin und Harman" *Berichte der Deutschen Chemischen Gesellschaft* 63: 120–125.

Späth, E. and E. Lederer 1930b. "Synthesen von 4-Carbolinen" *Berichte der Deutschen Chemischen Gesellschaft* 63: 2102–2111.

Speroni, E. and A. Minghetti 1988. "Neuropharmacological activity of extracts from *Passiflora incarnata*" *Planta Medica* 54: 488–491.

Spruce, R. 1873. "On some remarkable narcotics [*sic*] of the Amazon Valley and Orinoco, Ocean highways" *The Geographical Review* 1(55): 184–193.

Spruce, R. [A.R. Wallace, Ed.] 1908. *Notes of a Botanist on the Amazon and Andes*. Two volumes. Macmillan, London, England. Reprint in 1970; Johnson Reprint, New York.

Stafford, P. [J. Bigwood, Technical Editor] 1983. *Psychedelics Encyclopedia*. J.P. Tarcher, Inc., Los Angeles, CA. Third Edition 1992.

Stamets, P.E. 1978. *Psilocybe Mushrooms & Their Allies*. Homestead Book Co., Seattle, WA. Foreword by Gastón Guzmán.

Stamets, P.E. and J.S. Chilton 1983. *The Mushroom Cultivator: A Practical Guide to Growing Mushrooms at Home*. Agarikon Press, Olympia, WA. Foreword by Andrew Weil.

Sterling, B. 1992. *The Hacker Crackdown: Law and Disorder on the Electronic Frontier*. Bantam Books, New York.

Szára, S.I. 1956. "Dimethyltryptamin: Its metabolism in man; the relation of its psychotic [*sic*] effect to the serotonin metabolism" *Experientia* 15(6): 441–442.

Szára, S.I. 1957. "The comparison of the psychotic [*sic*] effect of tryptamine derivatives with the effects of mescaline and LSD-25 in self-experiments" In: Garattini, S. and V. Ghetti [Eds.] *Psychotropic Drugs*. Elsevier, Amsterdam, Netherlands. pp. 460–467.

Szára, S.I. 1961. "Hallucinogenic effects and metabolism of tryptamine derivatives in man" *Federation Proceedings* 20: 885–888.

Takagi, S. *et al.* 1979. "Minor basic constituents of *Evodia* fruits" *Shoyakugaku Zasshi* 33(1): 30–34.

Taussig, M. 1987. *Shamanism, Colonialism, and the Wild Man: A Study in Terror and Healing*. University of Chicago Press, Chicago, IL.

Thompson, A.C. *et al.* 1987. "Indolealkylamines of *Desmanthus illinoensis* and their growth inhibition activity" *Journal of Agricultural and Food Chemistry* 35(3): 361–365.

Turner, W.J. and S. Merlis 1959. "Effect of some indolealkylamines on man" *Archives of Neurology and Psychiatry* 81: 121–129.

Turner, W.J. *et al.* 1955. "Concerning theories of indoles in schizophrenigenesis" *American Journal of Psychiatry* 112: 466–467.

Tyler, V.E. and D. Gröger 1964. "Investigation of the alkaloids of *Amanita* species II. *Amanita citrina* and *Amanita porphyria*" *Planta Medica* 12(4): 397–402.

Udenfriend, S. *et al.* 1958. "Studies with reversible inhibitors of monoamine oxidase: Harmaline and related compounds" *Biochemical Pharmacology* 1: 160–165.

Ueno, A. *et al.* 1978. "Studies on the constituents of *Desmodium caudatum* DC" *Chemical and Pharmacological Bulletin Japan* 26(8): 2411–2416.

Uscátegui M., N. 1959. "The present distribution of narcotics [*sic*] and stimulants amongst the Indian tribes of Colombia" *Botanical Museum Leaflets* Harvard University 18(6): 273–304.

Uscátegui M., N. 1961. "Distribución actual de las plantas narcóticas [*sic*] y estimulantes usadas por las tribus indígenas de Colombia" *Revista de la Academia Colombiana de Ciencias Exactas, Físicas y Naturales* 11(43): 215–228.

Valadez, S. 1986. "Guided tour spirituality: Cosmic way or cosmic rip-off?" *Shaman's Drum: A Journal of Experiential Shamanism* Fall issue. pp. 4–6. Letter to the editor.

Van Beek, T.A. *et al.* 1984. "*Tabernaemontana* L. (Apocynaceae): A review of its taxonomy, phytochemistry, ethnobotany and pharmacology" *Journal of Ethnopharmacology* 10(1): 1–156.

Vickers, W.T. and T.C. Plowman 1984. "Useful plants of the Siona and Secoya Indians of eastern Ecuador" *Fieldiana* 15: 1–63.

Villavicencio, M. 1858. *Geografía de la República del Ecuador*. R. Craigshead, New York.

Wahba Khalil, S.K. and Y.M. Elkheir 1975. "Dimethyltryptamine from the leaves of certain *Acacia* species of northern Sudan" *Lloydia* 38(2): 176–177.

Walton, J.W. 1970. "Muiname diagnostic use of narcotics [*sic*]" *Economic Botany* 24(2): 187–188.

Wassel, G.M. *et al.* 1985. "Alkaloids from the rhizomes of *Phragmites australis* (Cav.) Trin. ex Steud." *Scientia Pharmaceutica* 53(3): 169–170. *Chemical Abstracts* 104: 48723f.

Wassén, S.H. 1967. "Anthropological survey of the use of South American snuffs" In: Efron, D.H. *et al.* [Eds.] *Ethnopharmacologic Search for Psychoactive Drugs.* [Public Health Service Publication No. 1645] U.S. Government Printing Office, Washington, D.C. pp. 233–289.

Wassén, S.H. 1979. "Was *espingo* (*ispincu*) of psychotropic and intoxicating importance for the shamans of Peru?" In: Browman, D. L. and R.A. Schwarz [Eds.] *Spirits, Shamans, and Stars: Perspectives from South America.* Mouton and Co., The Hague, Netherlands; Paris, France and New York. pp. 55–62.

Wassén, S.H. and B.R. Holmstedt 1963. "The use of paricá, an ethnological and pharmacological review" *Ethnos* 28(1): 5–45.

Wasson, R.G. 1957. "Seeking the magic mushroom" *Life* 42(19): 100 *et seq.* 13 May.

Wasson, R.G. 1961. "The hallucinogenic fungi of Mexico: An inquiry into the origins of the religious idea among primitive peoples" *Botanical Museum Leaflets* Harvard University 19(7): 137–162.

Wasson, R.G. 1968. *Soma: Divine Mushroom of Immortality.* [Ethno-mycological Studies No. 1] Mouton and Co., The Hague, Netherlands; Harcourt Brace Jovanovich, New York.

Wasson, R.G. 1977. Personal communications, Danbury, CT & Port Townsend, WA.

Wasson, R.G. 1980. *The Wondrous Mushroom: Mycolatry in Mesoamerica.* [Ethnomycological Studies No. 7] McGraw-Hill, New York.

Wasson, R.G. *et al.* 1978. *The Road to Eleusis: Unveiling the Secret of the Mysteries.* [Ethnomycological Studies No. 4] Harcourt, Brace Jovanovich, New York and London.

Wasson, V.P. and R.G. Wasson 1957. *Mushrooms Russia and History.* Two volumes. Pantheon Books, New York.

Webb, L.J. 1949. *Australian Phytochemical Survey.* Part I. CSIRO, Melbourne, Australia.

Weil, A.T. 1972. *The Natural Mind: A New Way of Looking at Drugs and the Higher Consciousness.* Houghton-Mifflin, Boston, MA.

Weil, A.T. 1980. *The Marriage of the Sun and Moon: A Quest for Unity in Consciousness.* Houghton-Mifflin, Boston, MA.

Weiss, G. 1973. "Shamanism and priesthood in the light of the Campa *ayahuasca* ceremony" In: Harner, M.J. [Ed.] *Hallucinogens and Shamanism.* Oxford University Press, London and Oxford, England. pp. 40–47.

Weiss, R.F. [Trans. by A.R. Meuss] 1988. *Herbal Medicine.* AB Arcanum, Göthenburg, Sweden.

Whistler, W.A. 1992. *Polynesian Herbal Medicine.* Nat'l. Tropical Bot. Garden, Lawai, HI.

White, O.E. 1922. "Botanical exploration in Bolivia" *Brooklyn Botanical Garden Record* 11(3): 93–105.

Wilbert, J. 1987. *Tobacco and Shamanism in South America.* Yale University Press, New Haven, CT and London, England.

Wilbert, J. 1991. "Does pharmacology corroborate the nicotine therapy and practices of South American shamanism?" *Journal of Ethnopharmacology* 32(1-3): 179–186.

Williams, L. 1931. "The death vine: Ayahuasca" *Field Museum News* 2(8): 3.

Williams, M. *et al.* 1971. "Characterization of alkaloids in palatable and unpalatable clones of *Phalaris arundinacea* L." *Crop Science* 11: 213–217.

Wolfes, O. and K. Rumpf 1928. "Über die Gewinnung von Harmin aus einer südamerikanischen Liane" *Archiv der Pharmazie und Berichte der Deutschen Pharmazeutischen Gesellschaft* 266(3): 188–189.

Zerda Bayón, R. 1915. *Informes Sobre Mi Excursión Científica en las Regiones Colombianas del Caquetá.* Bogotá, Colombia.

INDEX

[119]

ACKNOWLEDGEMENTS

I am beholden to Dr. Robert Montgomery of the *Botanical Preservation Corps* for bibliographic assistance and many valuable discussions about *ayahuasca* analogues. I am also indebted to the following specialists who have shared information, research and insights: Dr. Jeremy E. Bigwood of Guatemala City, Guatemala; Dr. James C. Callaway of the University of Kuopio, Finland; Dr. Ronald M. Cook of *Biosearch Technologies* in San Rafael, California; Dr. herman de vries of Eschenau, Germany; Dr. Mark S. Donnell of Silver City, New México; Dr. Josep M. Fericgla of the *Universidad de Barcelona*, Catalunya; Dr. Jochen Gartz of Leipzig, Germany; Dr. Luis Eduardo Luna of the *Swedish School of Economics* in Helsinki, Finland (whom I also thank for the slide of Pablo Amaringo's painting which graces the front cover); Dr. Dennis J. McKenna of *Aveda* in Minneapolis, Minnesota; Dr. Edward MacRae of São Paolo, Brazil; Dr. Jonathon S. Miller of *Centro de Investigación de Bosques Tropicales* in Quito, Ecuador; Dr. Galo Pichama of Morona Santiago, Ecuador; Dr. Berta Ramírez of Los Angeles, California; Dr. Alexander T. Shulgin of Lafayette, California; Dr. Constantino Manuel Torres of Florida International University in Miami, Florida (whose photograph of *Banisteriopsis caapi* appears on the back cover) and Dr. Steven A. Van Heiden of Austin, Texas.

I thank Dr. Martín I.P. Vinaver of San Andrés Tlanelhuayocan, Veracruz, for the line drawings which appear on the title and colophon pages, as well as Harvard University for permission to reproduce the botanical illustrations on pages 8 and 32.

I thank Dr. Albert Hofmann of Burg im Leimental, Switzerland together with Dr. Richard Evans Schultes of Melrose, Massachusetts, for their continuing advice and inspiration—it is always a pleasure to interact with these two great pioneers.

Saving the best for last, I thank my dear wife Djahel Vinaver who "moves in soft beauty & conscious delight..." She taught me to kiss "the joy as it flies" and to live "in eternity's sun rise." This book is dedicated to her in honor of her 30th birthday.

[127]

This first edition of *Ayahuasca Analogues*
consists of five thousand copies, printed by Braun-Brumfield
on white 60 pound book recycled, acid-free paper,
with sewn-and-glued bindings for permanence.
One thousand copies were Smythe-sewn and casebound;
of which 200 boxed copies were signed and numbered
1–174 and A–Z [the lettered copies *hors commerce*].
Printing was finished in March, 1994.